This book belongs to ...

Stonbridge
3G Shoooch
Amiru Bose

# AWESOME QURAN FACTS

## A colourful reference guide

### Saniyasnain Khan

# CONTENTS

## DISCOVERING THE QURAN

## PROPHETS AND PEOPLE

## TEACHINGS AND COMMANDS

Research and Editorial: Mohammad Imran Erfani, M. Harun Rashid
Art Editor: Mateen Ahmad
Graphic Design: Slim Haokip
Illustrated by Gurmeet

First published 2013
© Goodword Books 2013
Goodword Books
1, Nizamuddin West Market
New Delhi-110 013
Tel. 9111-4182-7083, 91-8588822672

Chennai Branch:
82/324, Triplicane High Road
Triplicane, Chennai 600005
Mob. +91 9790853944

email: info@goodwordbooks.com
www.goodwordbooks.com

Islamic Vision Ltd.
434 Coventry Road, Small Heath
Birmingham B10 0UG, U.K.
Tel. 121-773-0137
e-mail: info@ipci-iv.co.uk
www.islamicvision.co.uk

IB Publisher Inc.
81 Bloomingdale Rd, Hicksville
NY 11801, USA
Tel. 516-933-1000
email: info@ibpublisher.com
www.ibpublisher.com

Printed in India by Thomson Press

# THE PROPHET MUHAMMAD ﷺ

# MORE ABOUT THE QURAN

# PLACES AND LANDSCAPES

# What the Quran is all About ?

The Arabic word 'quran' means 'recitation' or 'reading'. The Quran is the sacred book of Islam. It is an exceptional book, and not just an ordinary book written by some human being. It records the words of Allah. The Quran, being the true word of Allah, serves as an eternal guide for all humanity. The main theme of the Quran is the Creation Plan of Allah.

## 4. The Revelation of the Quran

One night in 610 A.D., when the Prophet Muhammad ﷺ was in the Cave of Hira on Mount Nur near Makkah, as he would remain deep in thought about the Creator of the universe and the meaning of life, the Angel Jibril (Gabriel) appeared before him and, for the first time, taught him some *ayahs* of the Quran, starting with "Read in the name of your Lord…" The Quran was revealed part by part at different times over a period of 23 years.

## 1. Arrangement of the Quran

During the time of the Prophet Muhammad ﷺ whenever a part of the Quran (whether an *ayah* or a *surah*) was revealed, it was immediately noted down in writing by some scribe. The entire Quran was revealed in 23 years. After the complete revelation of the Quran, during the lifetime of the Prophet, once the Angel Jibril (Gabriel) came to the Prophet and put all the revealed *ayahs* and *surahs* in a certain order in which we read it till now. The arrangement was not in the chronological order of the revelation dates, thus we find the first revelation "Read, in the name of your Lord…" in chapter 96. *(Surah al-Alaq 96:1)*

## 2. Contents of the Quran

The Quran contains 114 chapters. Each chapter is called a *surah* in Arabic. Each *surah* has its own name, like *Al-Fatihah, Al-Baqarah, Al Imran*, etc. Every *surah*, with the exception of *Surah al-Tawbah* starts with the phrase, *bismillahir-rahmanir-rahim*, meaning "In the name of Allah, Most Gracious, Most Merciful". Each *surah* contains a number of verses which are called *ayah* (pl. *ayahs*). There are more than 6000 *ayahs* in the Quran.

## 8. The First Surah: Surah al-Fatihah

The first chapter or *surah* of the Quran is known as *Al-Fatihah*, meaning the 'Opening.' It contains seven beautiful verses beginning with praise of the Almighty Allah and a prayer for guidance to the right path at the end. These seven verses are also known as *al-Sab' al-Mathani*, or "the most oft repeated verses" as they are repeated several times in the daily prayers.

## 9. The Longest Surah: Surah al-Baqarah

The second *surah*, named *Al-Baqarah*, containing 286 *ayahs*, is the longest *surah* or chapter of the Quran. This *surah* has several narratives, such as the creation of the Prophet Adam عليه السلام, the stories of the Prophet Ibrahim عليه السلام and the Children of Israel, etc. It also contains several commandments of Allah. The longest *ayah* of the Quran also appears in this *surah* (*Surah al-Baqarah* 2:282).

## 5. The Shortest Surah: Surah al-Kawthar

The 108th *surah* of the Quran is the shortest *surah* of all. Its name is *Al-Kawthar*, which is the name of a fountain in Paradise, literally meaning 'Abundance'. It has only three short *ayahs* that give the good news to the Prophet that Allah has granted him the fountain of *Kawthar* in Paradise.

## 6. The Book of Guidance

Being the words of Allah, the Quran shows us the right path and prevents us from taking the wrong path. It teaches us the benefits of living a virtuous life and warns us against going astray. It acts as a spiritual and moral guide for mankind, making them conscious of their Creator – Allah and His creation plan.

## 7. Studying the Quran

Reciting the Quran in Arabic is a form of worship. But the real benefit of reading the Quran can be achieved if one understands its meaning. So, it is very important to read its translation as well, so that one can understand the meanings and messages of the Quran and also reflect on them. This is called *tadabbur*.

Interesting Facts ❯❯

# Interesting Facts about the Quran

In the 18th chapter of the Quran, it is mentioned that some believers, escaping from the tyrannous verdict of their contemporary king, took shelter in a cave along with their dog. By the decree of Allah, they slept there for three hundred or more years. And when they woke up, they found times had changed and they need no longer feel afraid. There were also a lot of admirers around them. This cave was discovered in the ruined city of Ephesus, Turkey (see *Surah al-Kahf* 18:9-22).

## 2. The People of the Cave

## 1. The Miraculous Words of Allah

The Quran is the most read religious book in the world. It is an exceptional book, and not just an ordinary book written by human beings. It is quite majestic in its style of writing and quite divine in its addressing of humankind. No human beings can produce such a book, even though they all get together to do so. Many things mentioned in the Quran have been proven to be true through modern science.

## 3. Allah Speaks to the Prophet Musa عليه السلام

One cold wintry night, on his way back from Madyan to Egypt with his family, the Prophet Musa عليه السلام lost his way in the darkness. Seeing fire burning on a far-off hillside, he went off to fetch a burning brand from it to give his family warmth. Nearing then it a voice to his right called out from above the tree: "O Musa, I am Allah, Lord of the Universe... come forward and have no fear; you are quite safe".
(*Surah al-Qasas* 28:30-31)

## 4. Pharaoh's Body

When Musa was made a prophet by Allah, he told the reigning king Pharaoh or Fir'awn to acknowledge God's truth, but Pharaoh refused. Finally, Pharaoh and his army were drowned in the raging sea. Of this event, the Quran says: "This day We will save your body, so that you will become a sign for your successors." *(Surah Yunus 10:92)*

A surprising prediction because when the Quran was revealed in the seventh century A.D., no one knew about Pharaoh's body. In 1898, the 3000 year old mummified remains of Pharaoh were discovered in the ancient city of Thebes thus proving the Quran's accuracy.

## 5. The People of Saba

Saba was an ancient country made fertile by the Marib dam which was very advanced for the times. The Sabeans were prosperous families of traders. But instead of being thankful to Allah and worshipping Him, they denied Him. Allah then sent a flood which destroyed the Marib dam and ruined their fields and orchards. Now only bitter fruits, tamarisks and a few lote trees grew there. The ruins of the Marib dam and some other monuments still exist in Yemen about 120 km to the east of San'a. *(Surah Saba 34:15-17)*

## 6. A Barrier between two Seas

In the 19th and 20th *ayah* of *Surah al-Rahman*, the Quarn says: "He has let free the two bodies of flowing water, meeting together: between them is a Barrier which they do not transgress." Modern science has discovered the truth of this Quranic statement. When the Mediterranean Sea waters meet the Atlantic Sea waters in the Gibraltar Straits, they do not mingle with each other but maintain the differences of their own qualities, such as salinity, density and temperature.

**Beautiful Commands** ▶▶

# Beautiful Commands

Kind words and the covering of faults are better than charity followed by injury.
(*Surah al-Baqarah 2: 263*)

O believers! When you give to others, give from the good things you have acquired; from that which We bring forth for you from the earth. Do not give worthless things which you yourself would not receive, except with your eyes closed.
(*Surah al-Baqarah 2:267*)

You will never attain righteousness unless you can give freely that which you love; and whatever you give, for certain, Allah knows it all. (*Surah al'Imran 3:92*)

If the debtor is in difficulty, allow him more time to repay till it is easy for him to repay. But if you pay it by charity, that is the best for you, if only you knew.
(*Surah al-Baqarah 2:280*)

O believers! Be steadfast in patience and constancy, compete in such perseverance; strengthen each other, and fear Allah so that you may prosper.
(*Surah al'Imran 3:200*)

It is only Satan that puts into your mind the fear of his supporters; Do not be afraid of them! Fear only Me (Allah) if you are true believers. (*Surah al'Imran 3:175*)

O believers! Believe in Allah and His Messenger, and the Book which He has sent to His Messenger, and the Books which He sent to those before him. Those who deny Allah and His angels, His Books, His messengers, and the Last Day, have gone far, far astray. *(Surah al-Nisa' 4:136)*

Serve Allah, and associate none with Him; and show kindness to your parents, to your kinsfolk; to orphans, to the needy, and to neighbours from your kin, and to neighbours who are not your kin, to the wayfarer, and to the slaves that you own; Allah does not love the arrogant, those who are full of self-satisfaction, nor those who are miserly or who encourage others to be miserly, or who hide the bounties which Allah has bestowed on them. We have prepared for those who resist faith, a punishment that steeps them in contempt. *(Surah al-Nisa' 4:36-37)*

Do not crave in any way of those things which Allah has granted more freely to some of you than to others; to men is allotted what they earn, and to women what they earn. *(Surah al-Nisa' 4:32)*

Give full measure when you measure, and weigh with a balance that is accurate; that is the most fitting, and most advantageous in the end. *(Surah al-Isra'17:35)*

If Satan tempts you, seek refuge with Allah, for He hears and knows all things. *(Surah al-A'raf 7:200)*

Your Lord has ordered that you worship none but Him, and that you be kind to your parents. Whether one or both of them reach old age in your lifetime, do not say to them one word of contempt, nor push them away, but speak to them in terms of honour; and spread over them humbly the wings of your tenderness, and say "My Lord! Grant to them Your mercy, as they raised me up when I was little." *(Surah al-Isra' 17:23-24)*

When the Quran is recited, listen to it with attention, and listen in silence so that you may receive (Allah's) mercy. And bring your Lord to remembrance in your very soul, with humility and with reverence, without raising your voice, in the mornings and evenings, and do not be negligent. *(Surah al-Anfal 7:204-205)*

This is a Book which We have revealed as a blessing; so follow it and be righteous, so that you may receive mercy. *(Surah al-An'am 6:155)*

And do not walk about on the earth with insolence; for you cannot rend the earth asunder nor can you rival the mountains in height. *(Surah al-Isra' 17:37)*

Be moderate in your pace, and lower your voice, for the harshest of sounds without doubt is the braying of an ass! *(Surah Luqman 31:19)*

# Beautiful Promises

They say, 'The Fire is not going to touch us, and [even if it does], it will only be for a few days!' Say [to them], 'Have you received a promise from God—for God never breaks His promise—or do you attribute something to God which you do not know? *(Surah al-Baqarah 2:80)*

We said, 'Go down, all of you, from here: then when guidance comes to you from Me, anyone who follows My guidance will have no fear, nor will they grieve— *(Surah al-Baqarah 2:38)*

But those who have faith and work righteousness, they are Companions of the Garden; therein they shall abide (for ever). *(Surah al-Baqarah 2:82)*

So remember Me; I will remember you. Be thankful to Me and do not be ungrateful. *(Surah al-Baqarah 2:152)*

God is the patron of the faithful. He leads them from darkness to the light. As for those who deny the truth, their supporter is Satan, who brings them out of light into darkness. They are the heirs of the Fire, and there they will remain forever. *(Surah al-Baqarah 2:257)*

It is not your responsibility to make them follow the right path; God guides whomever He pleases. Whatever wealth you spend is to your own benefit, provided that you spend only to seek the favour of God. Whatever wealth you spend [for God's cause] shall be repaid to you in full and you shall not be wronged. *(Surah al-Baqarah 2:272)*

Satan threatens you with the prospect of poverty and commands you to do foul deeds. But God promises His forgiveness and His bounty. God is bountiful and all knowing. *(Surah al-Baqarah 2:268)*

For, if you do not do so, then know that you are at war with God and His Messenger. But if you repent, you may retain your capital. Do not wrong [others] and you will not be wronged. *(Surah al-Baqarah 2:279)*

Those who believe, do good deeds, attend to their prayers and engage in almsgiving, shall be rewarded by their Lord and shall have no fear, nor shall they grieve. *(Surah al-Baqarah 2:277)*

They swear their strongest oaths by God that God will never raise the dead to life—nonetheless, it is a promise truly binding on Him, even though most people do not realize it— *(Surah al-Nahl 16:38)*

Surely, with every hardship there is ease. *(Surah al-Sharh 94:6)*

As for those who have believed and do good works, they shall be given their reward in full. God does not love evil-doers. *(Surah al'Imran 3:57)*

If God helps you, none can overcome you, but if He withdraws His help from you, who is there who can help you besides Him? In God, then, let the believers place their trust! *(Surah al'Imran 3:160)*

This Quran is an exposition for the people and a guidance and admonition for those who fear God. And do not become faint of heart, nor grieve—you will have the upper hand, if you are believers— *(Surah al'Imran 3:138-139)*

But God undertakes to accept repentance only from those who do evil out of ignorance and those who repent soon after. God turns towards such people with mercy; He is all knowing and all wise. *(Surah al-Nisa 4:17)*

That makes it more likely that people will bear true witness, or else they will fear that their oaths will be contradicted by the oaths of others. Heed God and listen; God does not guide a rebellious, disobedient people. *(Surah al-Ma'idah 5:108)*

Whoever does a good deed will be repaid tenfold, but those who do a bad deed will only be repaid with its equivalent and they shall not be wronged. *(Surah al-An'am 6:160)*

That which you are promised shall surely come to pass and you cannot prevent it. *(Surah al-An'am 6:134)*

Not so those who are patient and do good deeds. They shall have forgiveness and a great reward. *(Surah Hud 11:11)*

Prepare any strength you can muster against them, and any cavalry with which you can overawe God's enemy and your own enemy as well, and others besides them whom you do not know, but who are known to God. Anything you spend in the way of God will be repaid to you in full. You will not be wronged. *(Surah al-Anfal 8:60)*

If you tried to count God's blessings, you would never be able to number them. God is ever forgiving and most merciful. *(Surah al-Nahl 6:18)*

# Beautiful Prayers

O my Lord! Increase my knowledge. *(Surah Ta Ha 20:114)*

When My servants ask you about Me, say that I am near. I respond to the call of one who calls, whenever he calls to Me: let them, then, respond to Me, and believe in Me, so that they may be rightly guided. *(Surah al-Baqarah 2:186)*

But there are others who pray, "Our Lord, grant us good in this world as well as good in the world to come, and protect us from the torment of the Fire." *(Surah al-Baqarah 2:201)*

God does not charge a soul with more than it can bear. It shall be requited for whatever good and whatever evil it has done. [They pray], "Our Lord, do not take us to task if we forget or make a mistake! Our Lord, do not place on us a burden like the one You placed on those before us! Our Lord, do not place on us a burden we have not the strength to bear! Pardon us; and forgive us; and have mercy on us. You are our Lord and Sustainer, so help us against those who deny the truth." *(Surah al-Baqarah 2:286)*

Our Lord! Grant us what You have promised to us through Your messengers, and do not humiliate us on the Day of Resurrection. Surely, You never fail to fulfill Your promise. *(Surah al'Imran 3:194)*

They replied, "Our Lord, we have wronged our souls: if You do not forgive us and have mercy on us, we shall be among the lost." *(Surah al-A'raf 7:23)*

You would punish us only because we believed in the signs of our Lord when they were shown to us. Our Lord, pour patience upon us, and cause us to die in a state of submission to You. *(Surah al-A'raf 7:126)*

Then do not place me, Lord, with the wrongdoers. *(Surah al-Mu'minun 23:94)*

They said, "In Allah we put our trust. Our Lord, make us not a trial [the subject of persecution] for the oppressors. And deliver us by Your mercy from the people who deny the truth." *(Surah Yunus 10:85-86)*

Forgive me, Lord, and forgive my parents and all the believers on the Day of Reckoning. *(Surah Ibrahim 14:41)*

All they said was, "Our Lord, forgive us our sins and our excesses. Make our feet firm, and help us against those who deny the truth," *(Surah al'Imran 3:147)*

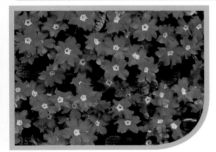

And say, "My Lord, I seek refuge with You from the prompting of the devils. I seek refuge with You, Lord, lest they should come near me." *(Surah al-Mu'minun 23:97-98)*

Say, "Lord, forgive us and have mercy. You are the best of those who show mercy." *(Surah al-Mu'minun 23:118)*

Who say, "Our Lord, ward off from us the punishment of Hell, for its punishment is a dreadful torment to suffer. Indeed, it is an evil abode and evil dwelling-place."*(Surah al-Furqan 25:65-66)*

My Lord, bestow wisdom upon me; unite me with the righteous; *(Surah al-Shu'ara' 26:83)*

Solomon smiled broadly at its words and said, "Lord, inspire me to be thankful for the blessings You have granted me and my parents, and to do good deeds that please You; and include me, by Your grace, among Your righteous servants!" *(Surah al-Naml 27:19)*

We have enjoined on man kindness to his parents: his mother bore him, in pain and in pain she gave birth to him, and his bearing and weaning takes thirty months. At length, when he reaches the age of full maturity and attains forty years, he says, "O my Lord! Help me to be grateful for Your favours which You have bestowed upon me, and upon both my parents, and to do good deeds that will please You. Grant me righteousness in my offspring. Truly, I have turned to You and, truly, I submit to You." *(Surah al-Ahqaf 46:15)*

Prophets Mentio

# Prophets Mentioned in the Quran

### ❶ The Prophet Adam علیه السّلام

Allah created the first man, the Prophet Adam علیه السّلام, from clay and gave him knowledge of all things. Allah also created Hawwa (Eve), as his companion, and asked them to dwell in the Garden and eat whatever they liked. But, tempted by Satan, they ate from the forbidden tree. So, Allah ordered them to descend to the earth and told them that those who followed the true path would enter Paradise, while those who followed Satan would be punished.

### ❷ The Prophet Isa علیه السّلام

When Maryam gave birth to the Prophet Isa علیه السّلام (Jesus) without a father, she was taunted for this, but Allah intervened, by endowing the newborn baby with speech. He said, "I am Allah's servant. Allah has given me the Book, and has made me a prophet." *(Surah Maryam 19:30)* Allah gave him the miraculous ability to cure the blind and lepers; and bring the dead to life. Later, the people, turning against him, decided to crucify him, but Allah saved him, while the people, by a miracle of Allah, crucified another in his place.

### ❸ The Prophet Yunus علیه السّلام

The Prophet Yunus علیه السّلام was sent to the people of Nineveh to call them to the one God. But, ignoring him, they continued to worship false gods. Finally, warning them of Allah's punishment, he left Nineveh aboard a small ship. Unfortunately, when the ship faced a violent storm, his fellow passengers thought him as their ill-luck and, threw him overboard and he was swallowed by a huge fish. Now, realizing his haste in asking for his people to be punished, he admitted his mistake and praised Allah from inside the fish's dark, suffocating stomach. Allah, hearing his prayer, saved him.

### ❹ The Prophet Ibrahim علیه السّلام

Born in Ur, Iraq, the Prophet Ibrahim علیه السّلام, chosen as Allah's messenger, spoke out against idol worship. This angered the king, Namrud (Nimrod), who decided to kill him. Nevertheless, he remained unscathed and preached Allah's message throughout his country. Later, he travelled to Syria, Palestine and Egypt. He travelled to Makkah also where he settled his wife Hajar and son the Prophet Ismail علیه السّلام. When the Prophet Ismail علیه السّلام grew up, they were ordered by Allah to build the House of Allah — the Kabah.

### ❺ The Prophet Yusuf علیه السّلام

When the Prophet Yusuf علیه السّلام, son of the Prophet Yaqub علیه السّلام, who lived in Canaan, was a child, he was thrown by his ten jealous step brothers into a dry well but was saved by a passing caravan. He ended up as a slave in Egypt, and once, when the king called upon Yusuf to interpret an unusual dream, he was so impressed by Yusuf's interpretation that he appointed him the Controller of granaries. Later, the Prophet Yusuf علیه السّلام invited his father and all his brothers to stay with him.

## 6 The Prophet Sulayman عَلَيْهِ السَّلَام

The Prophet Sulayman عَلَيْهِ السَّلَام (Solomon) ruled over Jerusalem as his father, the Prophet Dawud عَلَيْهِ السَّلَام (David), had done. Allah gave him power over the winds and the jinn, and the ability to understand the language of the birds, beasts, and insects. Never arrogant, he always thanked Allah for these blessings. Once a hoopoe told him about Bilqis, the Queen of Saba (Sheba), who did not believe in Allah. He wrote to her, inviting her to accept the true faith, to which she responded positively and submitted to Allah's true religion.

## 7 The Prophet Musa عَلَيْهِ السَّلَام

The Prophet Musa عَلَيْهِ السَّلَام (Moses), sent to the Children of Israel by Allah, was asked by Him to preach the oneness of Allah to Pharaoh, the king of Egypt and his people. But Pharaoh and his courtiers cruelly rejected him and his brother the Prophet Harun عَلَيْهِ السَّلَام (Aaron). Finally, Allah asked the Prophet Musa عَلَيْهِ السَّلَام to lead his people out of Egypt. Pharaoh and his huge army pursued them but the Prophet Musa عَلَيْهِ السَّلَام and his followers miraculously crossed the Red Sea, while Pharaoh and his army were drowned in it.

## 8 The Prophet Nuh عَلَيْهِ السَّلَام

The Prophet Nuh عَلَيْهِ السَّلَام (Noah) was sent by Allah to proclaim the message of His unity to his non-believing tribe. The Prophet Nuh عَلَيْهِ السَّلَام did so in public and in private for nine hundred and fifty years, but with little success. At last, he prayed Allah to punish these people. Allah then sent a flood which submerged everything, except Nuh's ark. After all the bad people had been drowned, the flood abated and Nuh's ark came to rest on Mount Judi, delivering the believers safely.

## 9 The Prophet Ayyub عَلَيْهِ السَّلَام

The Prophet Ayyub عَلَيْهِ السَّلَام (Job) was one of the great prophets of Allah, born in Damascus, Syria. He was a rich and prosperous man and had immense faith in Allah. People felt that the Prophet Ayyub عَلَيْهِ السَّلَام was such a faithful follower of Allah because of his riches and that if his blessings were taken away, he would not remain as faithful and grateful to Allah. Allah put him to a test by destroying all his riches, servants and family and afflicted him with an illness which lasted for 18 years. But he remained patient and held fast to his faith in Allah. All this pleased Allah and He rewarded him more than before.

## 10 The Prophet Salih عَلَيْهِ السَّلَام

The Prophet Salih عَلَيْهِ السَّلَام was sent to the tribe of Thamud who were prosperous builders and architects of their time, but without faith in Allah. He asked them to worship the one Allah, but they ignored him. One day, as a test, he asked them to allow a she-camel, sent by Allah, to graze and drink. But they killed her and were then severely punished by Allah's sending them a terrible earthquake which buried them all in their own fortress-like houses. Only the Prophet Salih عَلَيْهِ السَّلَام and his followers were saved.

## 11 The Prophet Hud عَلَيْهِ السَّلَام

The Prophet Hud was sent by Allah to the people of 'Ad. He was the first person to speak Arabic. Iram was the capital of the 'Ad people. At that time there was no city like it. Its inhabitants were great builders and made good irrigation canals in the vast tracts of sands. But many other tribes they became proud, obstinate and fell into evil ways. The Prophet Hud عَلَيْهِ السَّلَام asked them to give their wrong ways and to worship Allah, but they mocked at him. As a punishment Allah sent a storm that lasted for seven nights and eight days and completely destroyed them.

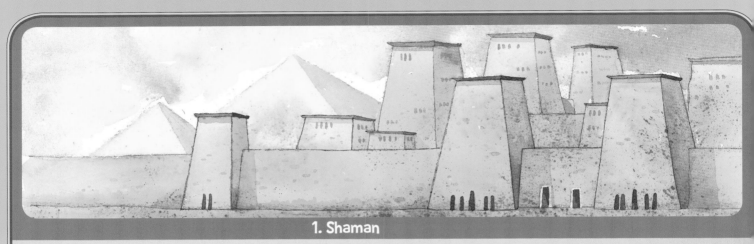

**1. Shaman**

Shaman was a secret believer in the message of the Prophet Musa عليه السلام (Moses) in the Firawn (Pharaoh) household. In the Quran he is called 'the believing man'. After the Prophet Musa عليه السلام had preached to Firawn and has certain amount of success, Firawn and his people planned to take the life of the Prophet Musa عليه السلام. At that moment Shaman tried to dissuade Firawn from killing him. He argued that it was not correct to kill a man just because he believed in Allah, especially when he was of good character and behaviour.

**2. Al-Khidr**

Al-Khidr (the green one) is described in the Quran as one of Allah's servants who was gifted with His mercy and knowledge. Due to these gifts from Allah he could also bring about changes in the affairs of the world. The Prophet Musa عليه السلام (Moses) was asked by Allah to travel to the union of the seas and to meet Al-Khidr, so that he could share some knowledge with the Prophet Musa عليه السلام.

**3. Luqman-The Wise**

The Quran tells of how Luqman, a man of wisdom, advised his son to worship none besides Allah; to be kind to his parents; to say his prayers regularly; to enjoin good and forbid evil; to be ever patient; not to be proud and arrogant; and to be moderate in gait and speech. He also told his son that Allah was All-seeing. We should all follow Luqman's wise advice to his son, so that we may become good human beings.

### 4. The Queen of Saba

When the Prophet Sulayman ﷺ came to know about how Bilqis, the Queen of Saba, and her people worshipped the sun instead of Allah, he sent a letter inviting them to worship Allah alone. To avoid any kind of conflict, the queen sent him gifts. When the Prophet Sulayman ﷺ did not accept them, she realized the authenticity of the Prophet Sulayman's ﷺ message. Along with her people she went forth to meet the Prophet Sulayman ﷺ and submitted herself to Allah.

### 5. Maryam

The Quran frequently mentions Maryam (Mary), the mother of the Prophet 'Isa ﷺ (Jesus), as an example for the believers of all times and exalts her above the entire womankind. Surah 19, which is named after her, gives details of her life. Calling her siddiqah (the truthful), the Quran clears her of the charges of unchastity levelled at her by the Children of Israel when she gave birth to the Prophet Isa ﷺ without a father.

### 6. Asiyah

Asiyah was the believing wife of Firawn (Pharaoh). She believed in Allah and in His supreme power. She also believed that, like everything else, Firawn was also a mere creation of His. She prayed to Allah to save her from Firawn and his sins and grant her a place in Paradise. She was a kind-hearted woman. She picked up the wooden box containing the infant Musa (Moses) from the Nile. She begged Firawn for the child's life and also to be allowed to bring him up. He agreed and she brought him up as her own son in the palace.

### 7. Mothers of the Believers

The wives of the Prophet Muhammad ﷺ, raised in status by Allah in the Quran to that of "mothers of the believers", led a pious life, supporting the Prophet in spreading the divine message. Khadijah, the first Muslim and the wife of the Prophet Muhammad ﷺ, gave him total support in carrying out his prophetic mission. A'ishah, the daughter of Abu Bakr, another wife of the Prophet, was very famous for her profound knowledge of Islam and numerous hadiths (sayings of the Prophet) were related by her.

Evil Characters

## 1. Iblis (Satan)

Iblis (Satan) arrogantly disobeyed Allah's command to prostrate himself before the Prophet Adam ﷺ, saying it was because the Prophet Adam ﷺ had been created from clay. Allah then expelled him as an accursed and disgraced outcast. At Satan's request, Allah granted him respite until Doomsday. But Satan vowed because of his expulsion to become the enemy of mankind, attacking them from all sides. Allah said. "I shall fill Hell with all of those who follow you." *(Surah al-A'raf 7:18)* From that day Satan has been the enemy of humankind.

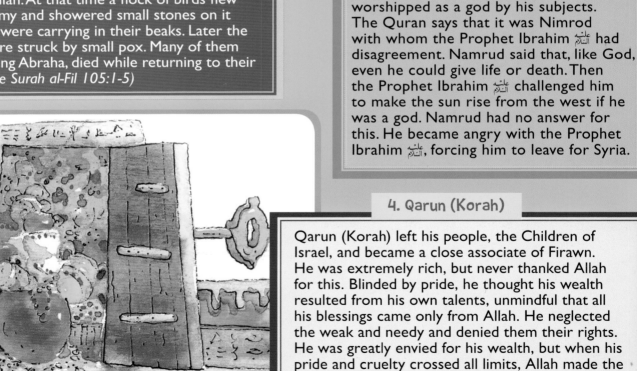

## 2. Abraha

Abraha was the Ethiopian Christian king who ruled Yemen in 6 A.D. He decided to destroy the Kabah and set out for Makkah with an army of sixty thousand of soldiers and dozen of elephants. The Makkans were helpless and unable to protect the House of Allah. At that time a flock of birds flew over the army and showered small stones on it which they were carrying in their beaks. Later the soldiers were struck by small pox. Many of them including King Abraha, died while returning to their country. *(see Surah al-Fil 105:1-5)*

## 3. Namrud (Nimrod)

Namrud (Nimrod) was the king who ruled ancient Iraq in the time of the Prophet Ibrahim ﷺ (Abraham). He was worshipped as a god by his subjects. The Quran says that it was Nimrod with whom the Prophet Ibrahim ﷺ had disagreement. Namrud said that, like God, even he could give life or death. Then the Prophet Ibrahim ﷺ challenged him to make the sun rise from the west if he was a god. Namrud had no answer for this. He became angry with the Prophet Ibrahim ﷺ, forcing him to leave for Syria.

## 4. Qarun (Korah)

Qarun (Korah) left his people, the Children of Israel, and became a close associate of Firawn. He was extremely rich, but never thanked Allah for this. Blinded by pride, he thought his wealth resulted from his own talents, unmindful that all his blessings came only from Allah. He neglected the weak and needy and denied them their rights. He was greatly envied for his wealth, but when his pride and cruelty crossed all limits, Allah made the earth swallow him up along with his riches.

## 5. Abu Lahab

Abu Lahab, an uncle of the Prophet Muhammad ﷺ, was also one of his most violent enemies. He tormented and humiliated the Prophet, and his wife strewed thorn bushes in his path. They carried on a non-stop campaign against him. Allah warned him that neither being chief of his tribe nor his wealth would save him from the fire of Hell. He and his wife knew of this revelation, but they persisted in their enmity towards Islam until their death. (see Surha al-Masad 111:1-5)

## 7. Pharaoh (Firawn)

Convinced of his own divinity, Pharaoh, enforced worship of himself. He mocked the Prophet Musa ﷺ and was cruel to the Bani Israil, whom he did not treat as equal to the Egyptians. He ordered all their male children to be killed, when a soothsayer predicted that a boy would be born into their tribes who would overthrow him. This boy was the Prophet Musa ﷺ, who was miraculously saved at birth by Allah. This all came true and Pharaoh was drowned in the Red sea while chasing the Prophet Musa ﷺ and the Bani Israel. Allah saved his body as a sign to mankind.

## 6. Samiri

Samiri, a member of the Banu Israil, misled the Children of Israel into worshipping a golden calf while the Prophet Musa ﷺ was away for forty days at Mount Tur (Sinai). Saying that the Prophet Musa ﷺ had forgotten his real god and also his people, he helped them to make a golden calf from their ornaments and asked them to worship it. On his return, the Prophet Musa ﷺ became angry at this. Samiri tried to flatter the Prophet Musa ﷺ, but this made the Prophet Musa ﷺ even angrier and he burnt the golden calf and cursed Samiri.

## 8. Abu Jahl

Abu Jahl, one of the leaders of the Quraysh and a dire opponent of the Prophet Muhammad ﷺ, tried to prevent him and his Companions from praying at the Kabah. Disturbed by his religious message, he was very jealous of the Prophet. Along with Abu Lahab and Abu Sufyan, he planned to kill him before the Migration. He also led a large army against the Muslims at the battle of Badr. Though the Muslims and many of the Quraysh were disinclined to do battle, Abu Jahl insisted upon it. He was killed in this battle.

# Tribes and People Mentioned in the Quran

## 1. The Helpers

*Al-Ansar,* meaning helpers, were the early Muslims of Madinah who gave great moral and material assistance to the Prophet Muhammad ﷺ and the *muhajirs* (migrants) after they migrated from Makkah to Madinah to escape persecution by the Quraysh. They played an important role in the history of Islam. Belief in Allah gave them such a strong sense of brotherhood that they were always ready to forego their own rights for the *muhajirs* and felt privileged in helping them. The Quran makes special mention of them along with the *muhajirs* as having earned Allah's blessings.

## 2. The Quraysh

The Quraysh, the noblest tribe of Arabia, to which the Prophet Muhammad ﷺ belonged, being descendants of the Prophet Ismail عليه السلام, the son of the Prophet Ibrahim عليه السلام became the custodians of the Kabah. Thanks to this custodianship and the location of Makkah, they became very prosperous. This was Allah's doing, but, when the Prophet Muhammad ﷺ proclaimed his message, they turned hostile and fiercely opposed it. When they failed to stop him, they started persecuting him and his followers. This forced the Prophet and his Companions to migrate to Madinah. *(see Surah al-Quraysh 106:1-4)*

## 3. The People of the Book

*Ahl al-Kitab* means the People of the Book. They are the people who were given the divine scriptures (books) before the Quran. In general, the Quran gives them a special place. There are some upright people among them who believe in Allah and the Day of Judgment and do only what is right. The Quran asks the Muslims to argue with them courteously and encourages discussions on mutually held beliefs. The Quran condems the ancient People of the Book for two main sins—rejection of the last Prophet (Muhammad ﷺ) and treating their preists as lord which is an insult to Allah.

## 4. Banu Israil

The Children of Israel (Banu Israil) were the people of the Prophet Musa عليه السلام who were saved from the tyranny of Pharaoh of Egypt. The Prophet Musa عليه السلام brought to them special laws, enshrined in the Tawrat (Torah). Allah bestowed on them many favours but, instead of being thankful, they became proud and started saying they were the sons of God and were the chosen ones. In the end, only a handful of them followed the teachings of the Prophet Musa عليه السلام.

## 5. Yajuj and Majuj

Yajuj and Majuj (Gog and Magog) were wild tribes of central Asia who used to attack people and spread corruption on the earth during the reign of King Dhu'l Qarnayn. To protect his people from their invasions Dhul Qarnayn raised an iron wall. The Quran says that when the Day of Judgement was near, Yajuj and Majuj would be everywhere on the earth. This would be a sign that the Day of Judgement was approaching. "When Yajuj and Majuj are let loose (from their barrier) and they swiftly swarm from every mound." *(Surah al-Anbiya' 21:96)*

## 6. Al-Asbat

Al-Asbat were the tribes descended from the Prophet Yaqub ﷺ and named after his twelve sons -- Rubil, Shamun, Yahuda, Isakhir, Yusuf, Misha, Binyamin, Hadd, Ashir, Dan, Naftali and Zabulun. When the Prophet Musa ﷺ led the Children of Israel into the Sinai desert, they thirsted for water but none was available. Allah then asked the Prophet Musa ﷺ to strike a rock with his staff, whereupon twelve springs gushed out - one for each tribe. By all accounts, this took place near Hareb, close to Mount Sinai.

## 7. Al-A'rab

*Al-A'rab*, or the desert Arabs of the Prophet Muhammad's ﷺ times, were mainly those living in and around Madinah. When Islam came to Madinah, several Bedouin tribes embraced it without really understanding or believing it. Some were true believers, others were weak in their faith and some were non-believers. The Quran says that, in the eyes of Allah, true *iman* (faith) comes when one discovers it as a reality and it touches one's whole being. Then one is ready to make every kind of sacrifice for its cause.

# Tales from the Quran

## 1. A Wise Judgement

The Prophet Sulayman ﷺ was the son of the Prophet Dawud ﷺ, a mighty king who ruled Jerusalem. Given wonderful powers by Allah, the Prophet Sulayman ﷺ as a child showed great wisdom. When two angry men came to see the Prophet Dawud ﷺ, one of them complained about the other's sheep entering his field and destroying his crops. The Prophet Dawud ﷺ sided with this man, saying he should take the sheep in compensation. But the Prophet Sulayman ﷺ made a better suggestion: to give the sheep to the owner of the field, who would use their milk and wool. Later, when the crops had ripened, they would be returned to their owner.

## 2. Sahib al-Jannatayn

Sahib al-Jannatayn were the owner of the gardens. Of them one was rich and the other was poor. The rich man had two big gardens which were full of fruits. He was proud and unjust towards the poor. He did not think that all that was a gift from Allah, but rather believed that they were the results of his hard work. The poor man tried to correct him that he should be grateful to Allah for His gifts. The next day, the rich man's gardens were completely destroyed by Allah by a rainstorm. He realized his mistake and cried for forgiveness from Allah.

## 3. The Prophet Musa ﷺ and the Magicians

About 4000 years ago in Egypt, Allah sent the Prophet Musa ﷺ with His miraculous signs to Firawn or Pharoah, the ruling tyrant, to convey His message. But Firawn dismissed his miracles as magic. Firawn then called his best magicians to outshine him. They threw down their ropes and sticks, which magically turned into serpents. Then the Prophet Musa ﷺ threw down his staff. This turned into a huge serpent which swallowed all the other serpents. Wonderstruck, the magicians recognized this as a true sign from Allah, and they bowed and proclaimed their faith in Allah.

## 4. The She-Camel

The Prophet Salih ﷺ, sent to reform the people of Thamud, having been rebuffed by them, tested them by means of Allah's own she-camel, who was to be left to graze unharmed, lest they be instantly punished. But, being great builders and architects, they had become very rich and also proud, so they just killed the she-camel, challenging Salih to bring down the threatened punishment. Salih told them Allah willed that they live only three more days. Unrepentant, they plotted to kill Salih and his family. But then Allah destroyed them all with a terrible earthquake.

# 5. The Great Sacrifice

One night, the Prophet Ibrahim ﷺ dreamt that, at Allah's behest, he was sacrificing his son, Ismail. When he told Ismail about the dream, being a fiathful servant of Allah, he willingly agreed to be sacrificed. For this purpose, the Prophet Ibrahim ﷺ then took Ismail to Mina a valley near Makkah. When Satan tried to stop them, they pelted him with stones. Pleased with this test of their will, Allah sent a ram through the Angel Jibril (Gabriel) to be sacrificed in Ismail's place and commanded the believers to observe this day as Id al-Adha, or the Feast of Sacrifice.

# 6. The Sabbath Breakers

Saturday was made the day of the Sabbath for the Children of Israel from the time of the Prophet Musa ﷺ (Moses). On that day, they were asked not to do any work, not even fishing, but only worship and remember God. On the Sabbath day, fish then came in shoals to the sea-shore. But greedy people would dig ditches so that the fish would be trapped in them. The next day they would collect the fish. In reality, they did not follow Allah's law, but only pretended to.

# 7. The Honoured Guests

One day, some angels in human form entered the Prophet Ibrahim's ﷺ house, saying, 'Peace! Peace!' Ibrahim did not recognize these strangers but returned their greetings and rushed to bring them a grilled calf. But the angels did not touch the food. Then the Prophet Ibrahim ﷺ felt afraid. But they said, 'Have no fear', and gave him the good news of a son who would become a wise person. His wife, disbelieving this, beat her face and cried: "But I am a barren old woman!" But the angels said that this was the will of the Lord, the Wise One, the All-Knowing.

# 8. The Prophet Shuayb ﷺ and the Earthquake

The people of Madyan, initially the followers of the Prophet Ibrahim ﷺ gradually turned away from the true faith, becoming dishonest in business and religion. They gave short measure and weight, denying others their rightful dues. Then Allah sent the Prophet Shuayb ﷺ to reform them. But they ignored him, denying both his prophethood and their wrongdoing. They even threatened to drive the Prophet Shuayb ﷺ and his followers into exile. Finally, they were punished by an earthquake destroying them all, as if they had never lived there.

# Islamic Expressions

## 1 Bismillahir-Rahmanir-Rahim

The Phrase, *Bismillahir-Rahmanir-Rahim* (In the name of Allah, the Most Gracious, the Most Merciful) is recited before doing anything, e.g. before taking meals, reading a book or beginning any new work. To commence any work in Allah's name is, in fact, to pray that Allah, the most Merciful the most Compassionate, should come to one's help and make one's work successful. In this way, man shows that he is the servant of the Almighty Allah.

## 2 Insha-Allah

*Insha-Allah* means God willing, or if Allah wills. The Quran commands the believers never to say, "I will do it tomorrow," without adding, "If Allah wills." Adding this phrase to such sentences means that the believer truly accepts the will of the Almighty about future happenings. While inviting his parents to come to Egypt, the Prophet Yusuf ﷺ (Joseph) used this phrase.

## 3 Alhamdu-lillah

*Alhamdu-lillah* means "All praises are due to Allah". This is a phrase used most often by the believers. This shows his satisfaction with and gratitude for the blessings and mercy which Allah has showered on him. It is also used on some other occasions, such as after sneezing; after drinking water; after the accomplishment of a task; after doing good deeds, etc.

## 4 Masha-Allah

The meaning of *Masha-Allah* is 'As Allah has willed.' This phrase is used while admiring something or someone, in recognition that all good things come solely from Allah. For example, if someone shows his friend the new watch he purchased, his friend should respond with "*Masha Allah!* What a lovely watch," thus acknowledging that the achievements and blessings are by the will of Allah.

## 5 | As-salamu-alaykum

This is the form of Islamic greeting, meaning "Peace be on you." The response is: *wa 'alaykum'ussalam* (*wa rahmatullahi wa barakatuhu*), meaning "and on you be the peace (and mercy of Allah and His blessings)." The phrase *'salamun alaykum'* occurs several times in the Quran. Allah says in the Quran, "And when those who believe in Our revelations come to you, then say: Peace be upon you!" The Quran urges the believer to respond more courteously and pleasantly to one who greets him. It says: "When a (courteous) greeting is offered to you, meet it with a greeting still more courteous, or (at least) of equal courtesy." This Islamic greeting shows that Islam is a religion of peace.

## 6 | A'udhu billahi min ash-shaytanir-rajim

This expression means "I seek refuge in Allah from the outcast Satan". In many places the Quran urges the believers to be alert and to seek refuge in Allah from Satan, the source of all evils. As he always tries to arouse evil thoughts in our mind, it is advisable to seek refuge from satan constantly, especially, when one is in danger of satan's temptations. We are also commanded in the Quran to seek refuge in Allah before starting to read the Quran. "So when you want to recite the Quran, seek refuge with Allah from Satan, the outcast (the cursed one)."

## 7 | Astaghfirullah

*Astaghfirullah* (I seek forgiveness of Allah) is an expression one uses when one feels guilty or wants to prevent oneself from doing wrong. The Prophet Muhammad ﷺ sought Allah's forgiveness more than seventy times a day. In fact, seeking Allah's forgiveness is one of the prominent signs of the true believers.

## 8 | La hawla wa la quwwata illa billah

This phrase means "There is neither power nor strength except with Allah." It is used to express denial of one's own claim to power and is an acknowledgement that all matters are ultimately controlled and decreed by Allah. The phrase is also spoken in such unfavorable situations as are beyond one's control and strength. In this way, by expressing his helplessness and powerlessness, a believer puts his trust in Allah, and submits himself to Him.

## 9 | Inna lillahi wa innailayhi rajiun

This means "We belong to Allah and to Him we shall return". This phrase is uttered upon hearing some bad news, e.g. a death, an affliction or a serious illness, etc. The Quran says: "Those who say, when afflicted with a calamity, "We belong to Allah and to Him we shall return (*inna lillahi wa inna ilayhi rajiun*)" are the ones who will have blessings and mercy from their Lord; it is they who are on the right path."

# Teachings of the Quran

## 1. *Dhikr* or Rememberance of Allah

*Dhikr*, or remembrance of Allah, is one of the basic teachings of Islam. *Dhikr* is a reality of nature. At every moment, man experiences those things which are directly related with Allah. All these things are manifestations of Allah's limitless power and might. So, it is but natural that all these things should be reminders of the Creator. Being influenced by Allah's creation, man's heart and mind produce divine feelings. *Dhikr* is nothing but the verbal expression of these feelings.

## 2. The Great Brotherhood

According to Islam, all human beings have been created by one and the same God, and for this reason belong to one great brotherhood. The teaching of Islam in this regard is that despite differences of colour, language, etc., people should harbor no ill-will towards those who are apparently not like them. They should promote fellow feeling towards others, bearing in mind that they are all traceable back to Adam and Eve. They should be each other's well-wishers and always come to one another's help.

## 3. *Tawhid* or the Oneness of Allah

Believing in the Oneness of Allah, or *tawhid,* is the central doctrine of the Quran. Believing that "there is no deity except Allah and that Muhammad is the messenger of Allah" is the first pillar of Islam. A Muslim should have the correct knowledge of his Creator and Sustainer. The Quran says, "He is God, the One, God, the Self-sufficient One. He does not give birth, nor was He born, and there is nothing like Him"*(Surah al-Ikhlas 112:1-4)* Ascribing of a partner to Allah is a major sin and shows utter ignorance.

## 4. Akhirah or the Hereafer

Man is an eternal creature. However, his life-span has been divided by Allah into two parts. A very small part of it has been placed in this world, while all of the remainder has been placed in the hereafter. The hereafter is a limitless world where all things have been provided in their ideal form. The present world is the world of action while the world of the hereafter is the place for reaping the harvest of actions. Those who prove to be God-fearing and pious in this world will enter into the eternal garden in the hereafter where they will enjoy all types of blessings. But those who are oblivious of Allah in this present world will be thrown into the fire of Hell.

## 5. Cleanliness of Body and Soul

Islam attaches great importance to cleanliness. A believer is a clean person and being so he should take extreme care towards his physical appearance as well as his soul. Allah says in the Quran: "Allah loves those who turn to Him in penitence and He loves those who keep themselves clean." *(Surah al-Baqarah 2:222)*

## 6. Tolerance and Forbearance

Avoidance of friction is one of the most important teachings of Islam. Such avoidance means refraining from retaliation on all occasions of complaints and dissension. Islam tells us that, on provocative occasions, we should adopt the policy of avoidance. That is, instead of behaving violently, we should opt for the course of tolerance, forbearance and non-voilence. Those who avoid friction and have patience will be counted by Allah among the possessors of superior character.

## 8. Keeping Patience

Patience is the exercise of restraint in trying situations — in Islam a great virtue — leading man to worthy goals. The Quran, time and again, advises believers to keep patience and not be deflected by adversity. The Quran says: "Surely, Allah is with those who are patient." When one experiences unfavorable situations, one should not be upset by them, but be tolerant and avoid reacting. The Quran says: "We shall certainly test you with fear and hunger, and loss of property, lives and crops. Give good news to those who endure with fortitude." *(Surah al-Baqarah 2:155)*

## 9. Respecting Others

Ridiculing others or calling them by offensive nicknames is a great sin in Islam. It strictly forbids people to make a laughing stock of others. The Quran says: "Believers, let not some men among you ridicule others: it may be that the latter are better than the former: nor should some women laugh at others: it may be that the latter are better than the former: do not defame or be sarcastic to each other, or call each other by offensive nicknames. How bad it is to earn an evil reputation after accepting the faith!" *(Surah al-Hujarat 49:11)*

## 7. Being Good to Neighbours

The Quran urges believers to be good to their neighbours. The Prophet Muhammad ﷺ once observed: "By Allah, anyone who is a threat to his neighbours is no believer." According to another *hadith*, he said, if a Muslim starts troubling his neighbours, his faith will become suspect. The relationship with a neighbor shows whether a person has human feelings or not, and whether he is sensitive to Islamic teachings. If one's neighbours are happy with one, that is a proof of one's goodness, but if one's neighbours are unhappy with one, that shows the very reverse.

## 10. Fulfilling Promises

Fulfilling promises is highly desirable in Islam. The Quran says: "Keep your promises; you will be called to account for every promise which you have made!" A believer should, therefore, be extremely sensitive about giving his word. Whenever he gives his word to anyone, he should make a point of keeping it. Readiness to fulfill promises is a commendable trait. It is a sign of a man's being the possessor the highest of human virtues.

# Akhirah or the Hereafter

## 1. What is Akhirah

The akhirah, or hereafter, is a limitless world where all things are in their ideal form. Death in this present world is not the end of life, but is rather the beginning of our real and eternal life. The present world is one of action, while the hereafter is where the harvest of actions is reaped. Those who are God-fearing and pious in this world will enter the eternal garden in the hereafter, to enjoy all kinds of blessings. But those who are oblivious of Allah in this present world will be thrown into the fire of Hell.

## 2. Doomsday

The earthquake of Doomsday will proclaim the termination of the period of trial. The freedom given to people in order to test them will be taken away. Then the time will have come for people to receive their rewards. The Quran declares: "When the earth is rocked in her last convulsion; when the earth shakes off its burdens and man asks 'what may this mean?'; on that Day it will proclaim its tidings, for your Lord will have inspired it. Thereupon, mankind will come in scattered groups to be shown their labours." *(Surah al-Zalzalah 99:1-6)*

## 3. Signs of Doomsday

One day, all the world, all of creation— human beings, animals, jinn, earth, skies— will come to an end. Nothing will be left except for Allah. The Prophet has foretold many signs that will appear before the end of this world. Some of them are: knowledge will be taken away and ignorance will prevail; intoxicants will be used widely; illegal activities will become widespread; adultery will become very common; earthquakes will increase; time will pass more quickly; tribulations will prevail; bloodshed will increase; trustworthiness will be lost; etc.

Teachings

## 4. Paradise

Allah has created an ideal world of everlasting joy and bliss called paradise. Those who obey God, despite their freedom, and voluntarily impose the will of God upon themselves, are deserving of paradise. During the period of man's trial, all kinds of people have been allowed to inhabit the world. However, when the trial of man has run its course, only the righteous will be deemed fit to inherit the evergreen world of God. Others will be denied entrance into heaven; they will be cast into a world of everlasting anguish and despair.

## 5. Hell

Hell, just opposite of paradise, is a place of everlasting punishment, prepared for the wicked. The Quran says how unfortunate are those on the Left: "They will find themselves in scorching wind and scalding water, and under the shadow of black smoke, neither cool nor refreshing." *(Surah al-Waqi'ah 56:42-44)* "You shall eat the fruit of the tree of Zaqqum, and fill your bellies with it, and shall drink boiling water. You shall drink it like thirsty camels." *(Surah al-Waqi'ah 56:51-55)* In Hell, the wicked will wish for death, but death will not come to them. They will eternally remain in this state of torment.

## 6. The Judgement Day

The Angel Israfil will blow the Trumpet, upon which all that are in the heavens and on earth will swoon, except such as it will please Allah (to exempt). This will be the end of all things. The Angel Israfil will blow the Trumpet for the second time, which will bring all the people to life. All of them will gather before their Creator, Allah, to be judged. The righteous will have their record in their right hands and the evil in their left hands. All will be brought to judgement and no secret will remain hidden.

Good Deeds

# Good Deeds

## 1. Forgiveness

Forgiveness is a pious act. The Quran teaches us to suppress our anger and forgive others' faults. "But if a person forgives and offers reconciliation, his reward is due from Allah: for Allah does not love those who do wrong." *(Surah al-Shura' 42:40)*

## 2. Hospitality

Hospitality has always been considered to be a great virtue concerning guests. In the 51$^{st}$ *surah* of the Quran, Allah mentions the story of how the Prophet Ibrahim ﷺ treated his honoured guests (angels sent by Allah to him). The Prophet Muhammad ﷺ once said that He who believes in Allah and in the Last Day should be hospitable towards his guests.

## 3. Honesty

Honesty covers to positive and virtuous attributes such as integrity, truthfulness and straightforwardness. Great importance has been attached to it in Islam. Allah says in the Quran: "O believers, fear Allah, and be in the company of the truthful." *(Surah al-Taubah 9:119)* Allah's Messenger said: "You must be truthful, for truthfulness leads to righteousness and righteousness leads to Paradise." Honesty, or truthfulness, is a virtue that distinguishes believers from hypocrites.

## 4. Modesty

Modesty is also a great virtue in Islam. In the story of the Prophet Musa ﷺ and the Prophet Shuayb ﷺ, the Quran mentions that one the two girls (daughters of the Prophet Shuayb) approached him (the Prophet Musa) "shyly". The Prophet Muhammad ﷺ said: "*Iman* or faith has more than seventy branches and modesty is a part of faith."

## 5. Chastity

It is a great virtue in Islam. Allah commands the Prophet in the Quran: "Say to the believing men that they should lower their gaze and guard their chastity: that will make for greater purity for them: And Allah is well acquainted with all that they do. Say to the believing women that they should lower their gaze and remain chaste and not to reveal their adorments– save what isnormally apparent there of." *(Surah al-Nur 24:30-31)*

## 6. Kindness

Another great virtue is kindness. The Quran says Allah loves those who are kind. According to a *hadith*, "Allah will not be kind to the one who is not kind to others." Besides human beings, the Prophet showed kindness to the animals as well. He is reported to have said: "Surely, there is a heavenly reward for every act of kindness to a living animal."

## 7. Truthfulness

The Quran says: "O believers, fear Allah, and be in the company of the truthful" *(Surah al-Tawbah 9:119)*. The Prophet Muhammad ﷺ says: "You must be truthful, for truthfulness leads to righteousness and righteousness leads to Paradise".

Bad Deeds

# Bad Deeds

### 1. Miserliness

Islam teaches its adherents to adopt the path of moderation. It dislikes miserliness as well as wasteful expenditure. In the Quran Allah says, "Allah does not love arrogant, boastful people who are niggardly, who urge others to be niggardly and hide the bounties which Allah has bestowed on them".
*(Surah al-Nisa 4:36-37)*

### 2. Arrogance

Arrogance is the offensive display of superiority or self importance. It was arrogance that caused Iblis disobey Allah. When asked what had prevented him from prostrating himself before Adam, he replied: "You created me from fire and Adam from clay." *(Surah al-A'raf 8:12)* The Quran mentions Luqman's precious advice to his son, "Do not avert your face from people out of haughtiness and do not walk with pride on the earth: for Allah does not love arrogant and boastful people." *(Surah Luqman 31:18)* About arrogance the Prophet once said: "One will not enter Paradise, if one has an atom's weight of arrogance in his heart."

### 3. Suspicion and Spying

Teaching us moral values, the Quran says: "Believers, avoid much suspicion. Indeed some suspicion is a sin. And do not spy on one another and do not backbite." *(Surah al-Hujurat 49:12)* In his sayings, the Prophet said: "Avoid suspicion, for suspicion is the gravest lie in talk and do not be inquisitive about one another and do not spy upon one another and do not feel envy for others, and nurse no malice, and nurse no aversion and hostility against one another. And be fellow-brothers and servants of Allah."

## 4. Showing Off

Riya, or showing off, is a bad habit. Allah does not accept the actions of those who do things just to show off. A believer is a sincere person. All his actions are meant to please the Almighty Allah. He knows very well that Allah is always watching him. He is Omniscient and Omnipresent.

## 5. Greed

Greed is an uncontrolled desire for money, wealth, power, fame, etc. Man wants to earn more and more so that he may accumulate more and more material assets. He remains immersed in that thought till the day he dies. After his death, man realizes that what was worth accumulating was something else. But the realization after death is of no avail. Therefore the Quran says: "And know that your wealth and your children are but a trail and that with Allah there is a great reward." *(Surah al-Taghabun 64:15)*

## 7. Backbiting and Slandering

Backbiting, or making hurtful comments about someone in his absence is a major sin in Islam. Likewise, slandering or giving false witness is equally condemned in the Quran. They sow enmity, and discord in the hearts of the people and cause their relations to be bitter and unpleasant. Allah says in the Quran: "And do not spy on one another and do not backbite. Would any of you like to eat his dead brother's flesh? No, you would hate it. Fear Allah, Allah is ever forgiving and most merciful." *(Surah al-Hujurat 49:12)*

## 6. Envy

Envy is an evil thing from which Allah asks men to seek refuge in Him in Surah(112) of the Quran. The Prophet Muhammad ﷺ warned the believers to beware of it, because it destroys good deeds in the way fire destroys wood.

## 8. Extravagance

Extravagance, or wasteful expenditure, is another bad habit. Those who spend their wealth in improper ways are called brothers of Satan in the Quran. Allah says: "And do not spend extravagantly; spendthrifts are the brothers of Satan, and Satan is ever ungrateful to his Lord." *(Surah al-Isra' 17:26-27)* Avoiding extravagance does not mean that one should become a miser; rather one should be moderate in one's spending and maintain a balance between the two.

# The Five Pillars of Islam

There are five basic religious obligations in Islam. These are:

**1.Shahadah**   **2.Salah**   **3.Sawm**   **4.Zakah**   **5.Hajj**

These five duties are known as the "Five Pillars of Islam" on which the religion of Islam stands. They are compulsory for every Muslim – man or woman. Without fulfilling these duties one cannot be a true believer.

## 2 Salah–Prayer

The *Salah* or the five daily prayers is the second pillar of Islam. They are: *Fajr* (Dawn), *Zuhr* (Noon), *Asr* (Afternoon), *Maghrib* (Sunset) and *Isha* (Night) prayers. After testifying the Article of Faith prayer is the most important among the four. Although prayers can be offered individually, it is encouraged to offer them in congregation, preferably in a mosque. Allah, in numerous places in the Quran, enjoins the believers to be regular in their prayers. The most important aspect of prayer is to bring people closer to Allah; to remind people constantly of Allah and His greatness; and to show obedience and thankfulness to our Creator.

## 1 Shahadah–the Testimony of Faith

The word *shahadah* means bearing witness, i.e., bearing witness that "there is no deity except Allah and Muhammad is the Messenger of Allah" (*la ilaha illallahu Muhammadur rasulullah*). By reciting this phrase, a man enters into the fold of Islam. This simple yet profound statement expresses a man's total submission to the religion of Islam. Discovering Allah along with His greatness and glory is not a simple matter. This is a discovery that effaces all feelings of superiority and arrogance from a man.

## 3 Sawm–the Fasting

*Sawm,* the third pillar of Islam, is observed annually throughout the entire month of Ramadan. The period of fasting lasts from the first light of dawn until sunset, thus obliging devotees to make radical changes in their daily routine. Fasting until sunset brings on sharp pangs of hunger and thirst which teaches the believer endurance and patience. In this way, believers prepare themselves to lead a disciplined and responsible life throughout the year. During fasting, believers try to refrain from undesirable things and engage themselves in religious activities, such as offering voluntary prayers, reciting the Quran, giving charity, etc. Fasting instills in a man, piety, or the fear of Allah; produces the spirit of thanksgiving; and infuses the spirit of prayer.

## 4 Zakah–Charity

The word *zakah* literally means purification. Here, it indicates purifying one's wealth by setting aside a portion of it for the poor and needy. In more than a dozen of places in the Quran, the believers are urged to give charity. Giving of charity or *zakah* is not just an act of worship it is also a religious method of managing social economy and just distribution of wealth. It purifies a person of greed, selfishness and niggardliness.

## 5 Hajj–the Pilgrimage to Makkah

Hajj or the pilgrimage to Makkah, is the fifth pillar of Islam. Affluent Muslims from all over the world gather once annually at Makkah, where the Kabah – the House of God– is located, to perform a special form of congregational worship in the month of Dhul Hijjah. The rites of hajj include circumambulation of the Kabah (*tawaf*), a brisk walk between the hills of Safa and Marwah (sa'y), visiting Mina and Arafat etc. It is such a complete act of worship that it has a salutary effect on all, whether in relation to Allah or to other human beings. Hajj is the supreme act of worship. To return from Hajj with one's faith in Allah strengthened and rekindled—that is the hallmark of a true pilgrim.

# The Prophet Muhammad ﷺ at Makkah

## 1   Birth of the Prophet

The Prophet Muhammad ﷺ, born in 570 A.D. in Arabia, belonged to the Quraysh tribe of Makkah. His father Abdullah, died two months before his birth. His mother, Aminah, although very sad, still felt strong and well as she waited for the birth. His grandfather Abd al-Muttalib, the head of the Quraysh tribe, guardian of the Kabah and protector of the visiting pilgrims, was very happy when the Prophet was born. He began to think of a name for the baby. Finally he decided upon Muhammad, an unusual name that means 'often praised,' or 'worthy of praise.'

## 2   Infancy

In those days in Makkah, it was customary for mothers to send their babies into the desert to be nursed by foster mothers from shepherds' families, and so the little Muhammad ﷺ spent the first years of his life with a woman named Halimah of the Banu Sa'd tribe. Her family was poverty-stricken but, as soon as Halimah began nursing Muhammad ﷺ, they began to prosper. They understood that this blessing was thanks to the baby Muhammad ﷺ, who grew well while with Halimah and her family.

## 3   Mother's Death

When Muhammad ﷺ was six, Aminah took him to visit his uncles in Yathrib (now known as Madinah). After a long journey by caravan, young Muhammad ﷺ enjoyed meeting his cousins and learning to swim. They happily stayed on for a month. But, tragically, on the journey back to Makkah, Aminah fell ill and died. Little Muhammad ﷺ returned home with Aminah's maid, Umm Ayman. After his mother's death, he was brought up by his grandfather, Abd al-Muttalib, and then by his uncle, Abu Talib, when his grandfather died two years later.

## 4   Marriage and Children

By the age of 25, Muhammad ﷺ had a reputation for his honesty, courage and gentlemanliness. On this account, Khadijah, a beautiful and wealthy widow of Makkah, employed him to trade her goods in Syria. Muhammad ﷺ did very well, earning greater profits than ever before. Moreover, Khadijah's servant, Maysarah, who accompanied him to Syria, gave a glowing report of Muhammad's superior character. Greatly impressed by Muhammad ﷺ, Khadijah married him. They had six children, two of whom, boys, died in infancy. The four daughters, Zaynab, Ruqayya, Umm Kulthum and Fatima, grew up into beautiful young girls and were married when the time came.

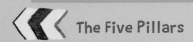

## 5 God chooses him His Prophet

The Prophet Muhammad's ﷺ marriage to Khadijah meant now leading a comfortable life. But soon, renouncing all worldliness, he began searching for the truth. Staying alone for days in the Cave of Hira, he would ask God such questions as: What is man's true role in life? From where does man come, and where will he go after death? Ultimately, the Archangel Jibril (Gabriel) appeared in human form and taught him the first revealed verses of the Quran. Surprised, confused and feeling unwell, he rushed back to Khadijah, who comforted him. She took him to her cousin, Waraqah, who reassured the Prophet that his experience had been genuine.

## 6 The First Beleivers

The Prophet Muhammad ﷺ, totally shaken by his first experience of revelation, came to accept his role as Allah's Messenger only with Khadijah's help. Khadijah was his first convert, next was his cousin, Ali and the third his foster son Zayd. The first unrelated convert was Abu Bakr, who became the Prophet's closest Companion. At first the Prophet taught Khadijah and a small group of friends how to pray, and they would pray together. Three years later, the Archangel Jibril commanded him to speak openly, and he did so at public meetings. Slowly the message of Allah began to spread.

## 7 Public Call to Islam

After three years of secrecy, the Prophet started preaching publicly, but with little success. The Quraysh tried to dissuade him from preaching so as to stop the message from spreading. So the Prophet Muhammad ﷺ was subjected to every kind of persecution. Thorns were strewn in his path, stones were thrown at his house, and he was pelted with dirt and rubbish. He was laughed at and ridiculed. Once, when he was praying in the Kabah, a sheet was thrown round his neck and pulled so violently that he fell on his face. His Companions too, faced all kinds of persecution.

## 9 The Year of Sorrow

During this period, the Prophet's uncle, Abu Talib passed away. Soon after this his beloved wife and greatest help Khadija died. Abu Talib was a respected elder of the Quraysh. Though not a follower of Islam, he had protected the Prophet against his enemies. Now, with the death of his uncle, the Prophet was without protection. His enemies cheered, and redoubled their brutalities.

## 8 Social Bycot

In the meantime the Quraysh had imposed a total social ban on the Prophet Muhammad's ﷺ family in Makkah. This period of boycott was one of great hardship for the Prophet's tribe known as the Banu Hashim, lasting for three years, and causing the family great suffering. Since all supplies to the valley were cut off, the Banu Hashim had to live on the leaves and roots of trees. Finally, certain kind-hearted Makkan leaders took pity on them. The agreement was annulled and the Banu Hashim were allowed to come back to their homes.

# The Prophet Muhammad ﷺ at Madinah

## 1 Migration to Madinah

The deaths of the Prophet's wife Khadija and his uncle in the 10th year of prophethood encouraged the enemy to persecute him. Nevertheless, the Prophet continued to successfully convey the message of Islam. This infuriated the Quraysh, for Islam was now also taking root in Madinah. Determined to crush the movement at all costs, they finally resolved to kill the Prophet. But before that, Allah, having a different plan for the Prophet, commanded him to leave for Madinah. The Prophet, therefore, accompanied by Abu Bakr, left Makkah for Madinah in the 13th year of prophethood.

## 2 A Warm Welcome at Madinah

As the Prophet and Abu Bakr approached Madinah, the people gathered, eager to greet them. Everyone wanted the Prophet to be his guest. Finally, at Allah's behest, he stayed with Abu Ayyub Ansari. Here, the Prophet spoke not of revenge but spreading peace, love and humanity. Those who accompanied him, the *Muhajir*, were treated as brothers and sisters by the Muslims of Madinah, the Ansar, who even shared their possessions with them. The Prophet's journey from Makkah to Madinah—the *Hijrah*, or migration—was the first real step towards the worldwide spread of Islam.

## 3 Battles at Madinah

The Prophet's departure to Madinah made the Quraysh much angrier. They did not want them to work in peaceful conditions. They now saw that the Muslims were all gathering in one place, and becoming increasingly stronger in the process, and so they resolved to wage war and crush them altogether. Consequently, they fought several battles with the Muslims during this short period of time. Most prominent of the battles of them were Badr, Uhud and the Trench.

## 4 Worldwide Invitation to Islam

The Treaty of Hudaybiyyah enabled the Prophet Muhammad ﷺ to focus on the other Arabian tribes and the Kings and Emperors of bordering countries. The Muslims could also return to Makkah for the pilgrimage; and although for only three days, they really impressed the local people with the simplicity and devotion of their lives, their kindness and respect for each other, and their love for the Prophet Muhammad ﷺ. Within just two years, the Prophet's followers rose from 1500 to 10,000, including several leading men of Makkah. This was the beginning of a new phase in the Prophet's mission to bring the divine faith to all nations.

### 5 The Peace Treaty

A peaceful atmosphere was essential to spread the divine message. The Prophet, a man of peace and reconciliation, ruled out war as an option. Therefore, in the sixth year of the *Hijrah*, he left for Makkah to perform *Umrah* accompanied by 1400 companions. He camped at Hudaybiyyah, just short of Makkah. His march was entirely peaceful, but the proud Makkan leaders, deeply resenting their visit to Makkah, barred their way. Here the Prophet signed a peace treaty with them, described in the Quran as 'a clear victory.' It provided for ten years of peace between the Quraysh and the Muslims.

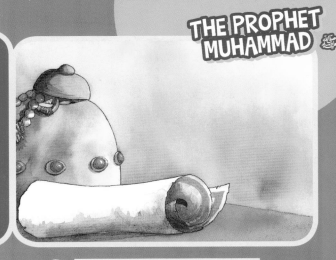

### 6 Conquest of Makkah

The Quraysh, regretted signing the Treaty and began breaking it by secretly supplying weapons to the Muslims' enemies. Aware of this, the Prophet Muhammad ﷺ realized that he must vanquish Makkah. To avoid bloodshed, he gathered a ten thousand strong army, aiming to scare the Makkans out of fighting. On the outskirts of Makkah, the Prophet ordered the army to kindle fires all around the city. This sight in the darkness would persuade the Makkans that a huge army surrounded them and that fighting was useless. This ruse succeeded. The capture of Makkah was, as planned, a totally bloodless victory.

### 7 A Forgiving Conqueror

The Prophet, unlike most victors, behaved with humility, entering Makkah with his head bowed and saying the victory was entirely Allah's doing. He then pardoned the Quraysh. Even Uthman ibn Talhah, who had once refused the Prophet's entry to the Kabah, was given back the key to the shrine. The Prophet and his followers then cleaned and purified the Kabah, and Bilal climbed to its top and gave the call to prayer. Even though now so powerful, the Prophet Muhammad ﷺ remained humble.

### 8 The Prophet's Final Hajj

In the tenth year of the Hijrah, the Prophet Muhammad ﷺ, accompanied by about 100,000 believers, set out for Makkah to perform his Hajj — commonly known as the Hajj of the Farewell (*Hajjat al-Wida*). Here he gave his famous 'Final Sermon', telling the assembled pilgrims to follow the Quran and his own example. Revenge and usury were to be ended. Property was to be respected. The Prophet then sought Allah's approval of his work and also asked his followers for their opinion. They replied: "We bear witness that you have conveyed Allah's message and have performed your duty and that you have meant goodness for us." He then asked Allah to be his witness. He ended by saying, "Let those present convey the message to the absent."

### 9 The Prophet's Death

During the sermon of his final pilgrimage, the following verse of the Quran was revealed: "Today I have completed your religion for you, and completed My blessings upon you. I have chosen for you Islam as your religion." This proved to be his last visit. That is why it came to be called the farewell pilgrimage. Only three months after his return to Madinah, the Prophet fell ill and breathed his last on 12 Rabiul Awwal 632 AD. The Prophet died in the room attached to his Mosque and was buried in the same place.

Sayings ❯❯

# Sayings of the Prophet Muhammad ﷺ

## 1. The Reward of Charity

The Prophet said, "If any believer plants any plant and a human being or an animal eats of it, he will be rewarded as if he had given that much in charity."

## 2. Truthfulness

The Prophet said, "Truthfulness leads to righteousness, and righteousness leads to Paradise. And a man keeps on telling the truth until he becomes a truthful person. Falsehood leads to wickedness and wickedness leads to Hell Fire, and a man may keep on telling lies till he is written before Allah, a liar."

## 3. The Reward of Serving Living Beings

The Prophet told of how a thirsty man got down into a well, drank its water and then came out. Meanwhile he saw a dog panting and thirstily licking mud. Seeing its plight, he went back down into the well, filled his shoe with water and from it gave the dog some water. Allah rewarded him for this deed and forgave him. The people asked, "O Allah's Messenger! Is there a reward for us in serving the animals?" He said, "Yes, there is a reward for serving any living being."

## 5. To Look After an Orphan

The Prophet said, "I and the person who looks after an orphan and provides for him, will be in Paradise like this." And he put his index and middle fingers together.

## 4. The Best Companion

A man came to the Prophet and said, "O Allah's Messenger! Who is more entitled to be treated with the best companionship by me?" The Prophet said, 'Your mother.' The man said. 'Who is next?' The Prophet said, 'Your mother.' The man further said, 'Who is next?' The Prophet said, 'Your mother.' The man asked for the fourth time, 'Who is next?' The Prophet said, 'Your father.'

## 6. Treat Your Neighbours Kindly

The Prophet said "Gabriel continued to recommend that I treat neighbours kindly and politely, so much so that I thought he would order me to make them my heirs."

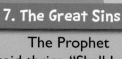

## 7. The Great Sins

The Prophet said thrice, "Shall I not inform you of the biggest of the great sins?" We said, "Yes, O Allah's Messenger." He said, "To join partners in worship with Allah: to be undutiful to one's parents." The Prophet sat up after he had been reclining and added, "And I warn you against giving a forged statement and bearing false witness. The Prophet kept on saying that warning till we thought that he would not stop.

## 8. A Good Deed

A man said, "O Prophet! Inform me of a deed which will make me enter Paradise." The people said, "What is the matter with him? What is the matter with him?" Allah's Messenger said, "He has something to ask about what he needs greatly." The Prophet said to him, "In order to enter Paradise, you should worship Allah and join none in worship with Him: You should offer prayers perfectly, give obligatory charity (zakat), and keep good relations with your kith and kin." He then said, 'Leave it!'

## 9. Beware of Suspicion

The Prophet said, "Beware of suspicion, for suspicion is the worst of false tales; and do not look for other's faults and do not spy, and do not be jealous of one another, and do not sever your relation with one another, and do not hate one another; and O Allah's worshippers! Be brothers as Allah has ordered you!"

## 10. He is not a Believer..

The Prophet said, "By Allah, he does not believe! By Allah, he does not believe! By Allah, he does not believe!" He was asked, "Who is that, O Allah's Messenger?" He replied, "That person whose neighbour does not feel safe from his evil."

## 11. Be Good to Your neighbours

The Prophet said, 'Anybody who believes in Allah and the Last Day should not harm his neighbour, and anybody who believes in Allah and the Last Day should entertain his guest generously and anybody who believes in Allah and the Last Day should talk about what is good or keep quiet. (i.e. abstain from all kinds of evil and dirty talk).

Companions ➤➤

# Companions of the Prophet Muhammad ﷺ

## 1. Abu Bakr Siddiq

Abu Bakr, the closest Companion of the Prophet, was only two years younger than him and a friend since childhood. He revered the Prophet so much that when he invited him to Islam, he unhesitatingly accepted. When the people of Makkah heard about the Prophet's Ascension to Heaven, they mocked him. But Abu Bakr said, "I would believe anything the Messenger of Allah said." When the Prophet learned of this, he called Abu Bakr Siddiq (truthful). Thus Abu Bakr earned the title of Siddiq from that day. Abu Bakr was also the first Caliph of Islam.

## 2. Umar ibn al-Khattab

Umar ibn al-Khattab was the second Caliph of Islam and a close Companion of the Prophet. He was foremost in matters of knowledge and learning. The Prophet conferred on him the title of al-Faruq. He was the first Muslim ruler to be known by the title of Amirul-Muminin. He was very famous for his justice.

## 3. Uthman ibn Affan

Uthman ibn Affan, another prominent Companion of the Prophet, accepted Islam in the early days. When the Prophet came to Madinah, he found that there was no source of fresh water in Madinah except the well of Bi'r Rumah, which belonged to a Jew of the Banu Ghifar, who sold its water to Muslims at high prices. The Prophet said: "Who will buy Bi'r Rumah and contribute it to the Muslims in return for a spring in Paradise?" When Uthman ibn 'Affan heard of this news, he bought it for thirty-five thousand dirhams, then he donated it to the Muslims.

## 5. Abdullah ibn Jahsh

Abdullah ibn Jahsh, a cousin of the Prophet, and an early convert to Islam, emigrated to Madinah with the Prophet's permission when the Quraysh's persecution of the Muslims became unbearable. Shortly thereafter, Abu Jahl occupied his house and distributed its contents among his tribesmen. Later, when Abdullah ibn Jahsh learned of this, he mentioned it to the Prophet. The Prophet said: "Aren't you satisfied, O Abdullah, with what Allah has given you instead — a house in Paradise?" "Yes, O Messenger of Allah," he replied, and never again complained about it.

## 4. Ali ibn Abi Talib

Ali, the fourth caliph and a cousin of the Prophet, was brought up in the Prophet's house from the age of five. In adulthood, he was respected for his courage, knowledge, and unflinching devotion to Islam. During his caliphate, his coat of armour once went amissing. It was found with a Jew in a market. Ali complained about this to the Qadi, who required Ali to produce two witnesses. But when Ali failed to do so, the Qadi decided in favour of the Jew. Seeing Ali's sense of justice, the Jew accepted Islam.

## 6. Abu Dharr al-Ghifari

Abu Dharr al-Ghifari, a Companion of the Prophet, abhorred polytheism from the outset. When he heard about the Prophet Muhammad ﷺ, he rushed to Makkah to learn about the new religion. There and then, he embraced Islam. He led a very simple life, shunning worldly goods and pleasures. Once a visitor asked Abu Dharr al-Ghifari why his house was so bare, and he replied, "We have a house in the Hereafter, to which we send the best of our possessions." Once the Prophet said that the earth did not carry nor the heavens cover a man more true and faithful than Abu Dharr.

## 7. Abu Hurayrah

Abu Hurayrah was the most prominent narrator of Hadith. He loved to caress and play with cats. Hence he got the name Abu Hurayrah - (care taker of kittens). After embracing Islam, Abu Hurayrah spent most of his time in the Prophet's Mosque looking after it and memorizing the sayings of the Prophet. Abu Hurayrah spent only three years in the company of the Prophet, but he narrated around 5,375 *hadith* during this short period.

## 10. Umm Sulaym

Umm Sulaym, mother of Anas ibn Malik, a famous Companion of the Prophet, was the first Madinan woman to accept Islam. She was a model Muslim woman with a strong and uncompromising belief in Allah who had devoted herself and all her belongings to the service of Islam and its followers. The Prophet frequently visited her and offered prayers at her home.

## 8. Abdullah ibn Umm Maktum

One day, the Prophet was engaged in trying to pesent Islam to the Quraysh nobles. When Abdullah ibn Umm Maktum, a blind man, interrupted him to ask about new revelations. The Prophet frowned and turned away from him. For this the Prophet was reprimanded by Allah: "For all you knew, (O Muhammad), he might perhaps have grown in purity or have been reminded of the Truth, and been helped by this reminder." Subsequently, the Prophet would often greet Abdullah ibn Umm Maktum, "Welcome he is on whose account my Lord has rebuked me."

## 9. Bilal ibn Rabah

Bilal ibn Rabah, originally from Ethiopia, was a slave of Umayya ibn Khalf of Makkah, one of Islam's direst enemies. When Bilal accepted Islam, his master tortured him severely by binding him and throwing the hot desert sand on him under the blazing sun. He bore all this but never renounced Islam. Later, Abu Bakr freed him from slavery. Bilal was the first Muadhdhin (caller to prayer). At an advanced age, on his death bed, he said to himself: "Tomorrow you will meet your loved ones, Muhammad ﷺ and his Companions."

43

# Prominent Mosques

### 1. The Prophet's Mosque

Al-Masjid al-Nabawi, or the Prophet's Mosque, situated at Madinah, is one of the three most venerated mosques. (The other two are al-Masjid al-Haram at Makkah and al-Masjid al-Aqsa at Jerusalem). Of the three sacred mosques, this mosque takes second place. When the Prophet Muhammad ﷺ migrated from Makkah to Madinah, he built this mosque from palm trunks, aided by his Companions. Later, it was continually reconstructed and extended. The Mosque contains the Prophet's tomb and the graves of Abu Bakr and 'Umar. Most of the Hajj pilgrims visit this mosque too when they travel to Makkah.

### 2. The Jumuah Mosque

Masjid al-Jumuah, or the Jumuah Mosque is situated about 2.5 kilometers south of al-Masjid al-Nabawi in Madinah. It was named so, as the Prophet led the first Jumuah (Friday) prayer here shortly after arriving in Madinah. After performing the Jumuah prayer, the Prophet mounted his she-camel and set off for the city of Madinah. It was constructed exactly at the place where the Prophet offered the prayer.

### 4. The Sacred Mosque

The most sacred mosque of the all, known as Al-Masjid al-Haram, or the Sacred Mosque, the Kabah and also Baytullah (House of Allah) is located in the city of Makkah in Saudi Arabia. It was initially built by the Prophet Ibrahim عليه السلام and Ismail عليه السلام more than 4000 years ago. Reconstructed several times since then, it retains its ancient form. Five times every day, more than a quarter of the world's population prays towards the Kabah. Millions of Muslims travel there annually to perform the rites of Hajj, which provides a focal point for the unity of the Muslim Umma.

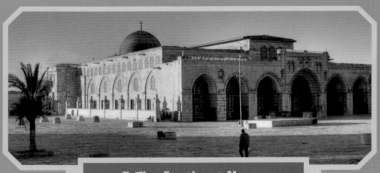

### 3. The Farthest Mosque

During the Night of his Ascension, the Prophet Muhammad ﷺ was taken to the site of the Temple of the Prophet Sulayman عليه السلام in Jerusalem (referred to, in the Quran as Al-Masjid al-Aqsa, or the Farthest Mosque.) Here he led the other prophets in prayer. Al Masjid al-Aqsa takes third place among the three sacred mosques, the other two being the Kabaah and the Mosque of the Prophet. For some time, the Prophet prayed towards this mosque. Later, he was commanded to change the Qibla towards the Kabah.

### 5. The Importance of Three Sacred Mosques

The Prophet Muhammad ﷺ said, "A prayer in Masjid al-Haram is better than one hundred thousand prayers offered in any other mosque and a prayer in my Masjid (Masjid al-Nabawi) is better than one thousand prayers in any other mosque and a prayer in al-Masjid al-Aqsa is better than five hundred prayers in any other mosque." The Prophet Muhammad ﷺ also observed, "Do not set out on a journey except for three mosques: al-Masjid al-Haram, al-Masjid al-Nabawi and al-Masjid al-Aqsa."

### 6. The Mosque of Al-Khayf

Masjid al-Khayf is located at the foot of a mountain to the south of Mina in Makkah. It is the place where the Prophet Muhammad ﷺ offered *salah* during his hajj. Pilgrims also pray in this Mosque during their stay at Mina. It is 25,000 square meters in area and can accommodate more than 25,000 pilgrims. From a distance, Masjid al-Khayf looks very beautiful with its surrounding tents where pilgrims stay for three days during the Hajj.

### 7. The Mosque of Nimrah

Masjid Nimrah is located on the plain of Arafat in Makkah. The Prophet camped here on the ninth day of Dhul Hijjah, during his farewell pilgrimage. After midday he delivered his last sermon at the Valley of Urnah being mounted on his camel, and then led the *salah* (prayer). More than 100,000 Companions accompanied him on this Hajj journey. During the second century of Islam, this mosque was built at this same spot. Here, the pilgrims perform their Zuhr and Asr prayers in congregation and then move towards Arafat to stay there till the sunset.

### 8. The Mosque of Quba

Upon his arrival at Madinah, the Prophet first stopped at Quba, a place 5 km (3 miles) away from the city, where the Prophet's she-camel, Qaswa', knelt down. The Prophet himself settled here for some time before moving to the city. Here he built the first mosque in Islam, which later came to be known as the Masjid Quba. It was built by the Companions and the Prophet himself took part in its constructions. The mosque is also known as the Masjid al-Taqwa (the Mosque of Piety).

### 9. The Mosque of Two Qiblahs

This is the mosque where the Prophet Muhammad ﷺ, while leading the believers in prayer, was asked by a revelation of the Quran to turn his face in the direction of the Sacred Mosque, the Kabah: wherever people were, they had to turn their faces in that direction. The Prophet, still leading the prayer, faced away from the earlier *qiblah*, which was towards Jerusalem, and turned in the direction of the Kabah in Makkah. This mosque lies to the north west of the Prophet's Mosque, and is about 3.5 km away from it in Madinah.

# Miracles

### 1 Table Spread with Food

One day, the disciples of the Prophet Isa ﷺ (Jesus) asked him whether his Lord could send down a table spread with food from the heavens. The Prophet Isa ﷺ warned them and pleaded with them to fear Allah, if they were true believers. But they insisted on their demand. Finally, the Prophet Isa ﷺ was compelled to request his Lord to fulfill their demand. In answer to the Prophet Isa's request, angels brought down a table spread with delicious food – a special miracle quite different from all others.

### 3 The Prophet Ibrahim ﷺ and the Fire

When the Prophet Ibrahim ﷺ proclaimed his message of monotheism, his people, who were idol worshippers, turned against him and wanted to burn him alive. They threw him into a huge bonfire, but Ibrahim felt no fear, as his faith in Allah was very strong and he knew the people were wrong. Allah was with him and commanded the fire to be cool and keep Ibrahim safe and sound. The fire bowed to Allah's will, and so Ibrahim emerged unscathed from it. The disbelievers were astonished.

### 2 A Baby Boy in the Box

When the Prophet Musa ﷺ (Moses) was born, Egypt's ruling Pharaoh or Firawn ordered all newborn male children of the Banu Israel to be killed. The Prophet Musa's ﷺ mother greatly feared Pharaoh's cruelties, but Allah allayed her fears, telling her to cast him into the river Nile in a box. She did so and, finally, the box floated to a bank near the royal palace. When Pharaoh's wife saw it, she had it retrieved from the water. When she saw the baby in it, her heart was touched, and despite the king's objection, the queen decided to keep the baby and rear him as her own child.

### 4 The Surprise of the Prophet Uzayr عليه السلام

The Prophet Uzayr عليه السلام had a donkey on which he used to travel. Once, while passing through the ruins of a city where no one lived, he wondered: "How can Allah give life to this city that is dead." Allah wanted to teach the Prophet Uzayr عليه السلام that He had power over everything. He there and then caused him and his donkey to die and then brought them back to life a 100 years later. Then Allah asked him how long he had stayed away. He replied: 'A day, or part of a day'. Allah said: "No, you have stayed away 100 years."

### 5 Birds Brought Back to Life after Death

To strengthen his faith, the Prophet Ibrahim عليه السلام once asked Allah to show him how He gave life after death. Allah then commanded him to take four birds and train them to return to him. Then He asked him to place each one of them on top of different hills. Next, Allah told him to call the birds. The Prophet Ibrahim عليه السلام did as commanded, called the birds and they immediately flew to him. This reassured him that one day, Allah will revive the dead and we all have to return to Him.

### 6 Fresh Food from Heaven

In the Quran, Maryam, the Prophet Isa's عليه السلام mother, is set above all other women for her piety and chastity. The Prophet Muhammad ﷺ called her one of the best women in the world. She grew up in the care of the Prophet Zakariyya عليه السلام, spending most of her time in the *mihrab* (prayer-niche) worshipping her Lord. But whenever Zakariyya went to see her, he found she had fresh food. When he asked her where this food came from, she would reply: "From Allah, Allah gives as much as He likes to whoever He pleases." *(Surah Al-'Imran 3:37)*

### 7 The Spring of Zamzam

When the Prophet Ibrahim عليه السلام settled his wife Hajar and baby son Ismail in Makkah, a barren, lifeless valley, Hajar's water supply ran out and Ismail began to cry with thirst. Hajar, seeking water everywhere, ran seven times between the hillocks of Safa and Marwah. Finally, atop Marwah, she saw an angel digging near Ismail's feet, whereupon water gushed forth. At this, she shouted 'Zamzam'— the Babylonian word for the sound of rushing water. Thus, Allah saved the life of Hajar and her son Ismail. Today millions of pilgrims regularly drink the water of Zamzam and also take it home with them.

Animals & Birds

# Animals and Birds

## 1  Sheep

The sheep is a domestic animal that gives us milk, flesh, leather and wool. In many places the Quran mentions this animal. In *Surah Sad* it describes the story of disputants who came to the Prophet Dawud ﷺ to judge between them fairly. One of them had ninety nine sheeps while the other had only one yet the former had the desire to have his one too.

## 2  Camel

The camel has been frequently mentioned in the Quran. Being a unique animal especially suited to the desert, it can go for several days without drinking water. The Quran urges people to ponder upon this amazing creature of Allah. "Do they not look at the camels, how they are made?" The purpose of this is that man reflect on their creation and give thanks to Allah for creating such wonderful creatures.

## 3  Dog

The Quran, giving an example of those who deny His Signs, says, "His similitude is that of a dog: if you attack him, he lolls out his tongue, or if you leave him alone, he (still) lolls out his tongue. That is the similitude of those who reject Our signs." *(Surah al-A'raf 7:176)*

## 4  Horse

The horse is an obedient animal. Since time immemmorial, horses have been kept by man as beasts of burden. They stood for power and were very important for the army and for travelling to far-off places. The Quran says, "And (Allah has created) horses, mules, and donkeys for you to ride and use for show." *(Surah al-Nahl 16:8)* The Prophet Sulayman ﷺ (Solomon) was very fond of horses.

## 5  Hoopoe

The Prophet Sulayman ﷺ (Solomon), by God's grace, was a very powerful king and knew the language of the birds. His army included birds, animals and jinn. Once, finding the hoopoe absent, (see *Surah al-Naml*) he became angry and threatened it with severe punishment if it failed to account for itself. But shortly thereafter, it brought news of the Queen of Sheba whose people were sun worshippers. Sulayman then sent a letter to the Queen of Sheba by the hoopoe (*hudhud*). On receiving it, the Queen came to the Prophet Sulayman ﷺ and submitted herself to the true faith.

## 6  Cow

The cow is a very useful animal for man. Man has always reared the cow for its milk. The Quran says, "And surely in cattle (too) you will find an instructive Sign. From what is within their bodies, between excretions and blood, We produce, for your drink, milk, pure and agreeable to those who drink it." *(Surah al-Nahl 16:66)*

**Miracles**

48

## 7    Donkey

In the ancient times, the donkey was a useful means of transport. It figured in several Quranic stories, such as that of the Prophet Uzayr ﷺ who, while riding on his donkey, was shown a miracle by Allah which affirmed his faith in the Hereafter. Luqman, while advising his son, cautions him to be modest, always lowering his voice, as the ugliest voice is that of the braying donkey. The Quran says, moreover, that those who study divine books without following them are like donkeys that carry loads of books without understanding them.

## 8    Raven

The Quran records the story of the two sons of the Prophet Adam ﷺ. When the elder bother killed his younger brother after a fight, he felt very sorry when his anger cooled down. He was not sure what to do with the dead body. So Allah sent a raven who taught him to hide the dead body of his brother by scratching the ground. Seeing this, Qabil realized his powerlessness: "Woe is me! Was I not even able to be as this raven, and to hide the corpse of my brother?" *(Surah al-Ma'idah 5:31)*

## 9    Quail

The Quran tells us that when the Prophet Musa ﷺ along with the Bani Israil journeyed from Egypt towards the holy land, Allah provided them with special food-- manna and quails. Manna, a kind of sweet dew, and the roast quails, a tasty dish, awaited them. This was a bounty of Allah bestowed upon them so that they had not to toil for their food. Yet, the Bani Israil were ungrateful. They complained about the sameness of the food and asked for greater variety.

## 10    Wolf

A dangerous and cunning animal, it attacks and feeds on smaller animals, but also attacks humans, especially children. In the story of the Prophet Yusuf ﷺ, his ten step brothers, being jealous of him, threw him into a dry well and lied to their old father that a wolf had eaten Yusuf. They also showed him his shirt with false blood on it.

## 11    Elephant

With their massive bodies and great strength, elephants were mostly used in royal armies. Before the birth of the Prophet Muhammad ﷺ, the king of Yemen, Abraha, marched towards Makkah with a huge army of elephants, intending to destroy the Kabah. But even before he reached Makkah, Allah sent a flock of birds to pelt the soldiers with small stones, so that they fell ill. Abraha was thus forced to return to his country and died soon after. *(see Surah al-Fil 105)*

Fruits & Vegetables ➤➤

# Fruits and Vegetables

## 1 Dates

The date is frequently mentioned in the Quran. It is one of the best nutritious foods for mankind as it contains sucrose, glucose, protein, cellulose, starch and vitamins A, B and C. Dates are also rich in natural fibres and, therefore, the eating of them helps to fight many ailments. One of its medicinal values is that it helps to cure respiratory disorders. The Prophet said, "If any one of you is fasting, let him break his fast with dates. In case he does not have them, then with water. Surely water is a purifier."

## 2 Olive

The olive is a popular fruit mentioned at several places in the Quran. It is cultivated in all Mediterranean countries. It can be eaten fresh as well as being used in many recipes. Its oil has great medicinal value. It is nutritious demulcent and is also a mild purgative. It helps with gastric and duodenal ulcers. The Prophet Muhammad ﷺ said, "Consume olive oil, and rub it on to your skin, because it comes from a blessed tree."

## 3 Fig

The fig, one of the ancient fruits consumed by man is pan tropic, fibreless, and a source of minerals and vitamins. It removes kidney and bladder stones and cleanses the liver and spleen. It also is helpful in long periods of recuperation. The Prophet said, "Eat figs. If I said a certain type of fruit was sent down to us from the heavens, I would say it is a fig, because it has no seeds. It cures piles and is useful for rheumatism."

## 4 Grapes

Frequently mentioned in the Quran, grapes are very popular fruits which can be eaten raw or used for making preserves, etc. It also has a number of medicinal values, being a source of glucose, fructose and minerals. The vitamin P in it checks the bleeding caused by diabetes. It increases and purifies the blood. Allah says in The Quran, "Then We brought forth for you therewith gardens of date-palms and grapes, wherein is much fruit for you, and whereof you eat." *(Surah al-Mu'minun 23:19)* Experimental studies have proved that grape seeds are also effective in fighting cancerous cells.

## 5 Pomegranate

This fruit, mentioned in the Quran three times, contains a maze of nutritious, sweet and juicy seeds and has many medicinal properties. It is a tonic for the heart, and helps to cure stomach inflammation, diarrhea, high blood pressure and anaemia, etc. Traditional medics prepared various liquids from its skin, flowers and even the stem of its tree. Modern, medical science has also discovered in it several medicinal properties. Once the Prophet Muhammad ﷺ said, "There is not a pomegranate which does not have a pip from one of the pomegranates from Jannah in it."

## 6 Cucumber

The cucumber (mentioned in *Surah* al-Baqarah) having a high water content plus electrolytes, has many health benefits. It helps in purifying the skin and reduces swelling and sunburn. A low calorie vegetable, its 96% water content is more nutritious than regular water, which helps in keeping the body hydrated and regulating body temperature. It also helps in flushing out the toxins from the body. The Companions have been reported to have seen the Prophet eating cucumber with fresh dates.

## 7 Onion

Onions, eaten raw, cooked or fried, are commonly used to flavor dips, salads, soups and other dishes. With their variety of health-giving organic sulfur compounds, they are used to treat different types of diseases. The onion is lawful for believers; however, if anyone eats raw or uncooked onion or garlic, he should not approach the mosque. The Prophet said, "He who eats onion and garlic and leek, should not approach our mosque, for the angels are harmed by the same things as the children of Adam."

## 8 Gourd

The Quran tells us that when the Prophet Yunus ﷺ, or Jonah, came out of the belly of the fish he fed on gourds to get nourishment. This plant protected him from the scorching sun. Gourds (*yaqtin*) contain vitamin B, C, calcium, iron and are useful in curing headaches and gout.

## 9 Garlic

Garlic is a plant with a very strong and bitter flavour which has been used for both culinary and medical purposes for hundreds of years. Garlic is known to have wonderful anti-bacterial, anti-viral, anti-fungal and anti-oxidant properties. Garlic is one of the most valuable and versatile foods and is a widely recognized health enhancing supplement. It is mentioned in the Quran in the story of the Prophet Musa ﷺ and Banu Israil in which they wanted to have these vegetables after becoming tired of *manna* and *salwa*.

# Things from Nature

## Rain

Allah says in the Quran: "We let the rain pour down in torrents and then We cleaved the earth asunder." Then He goes on to tell of the variety of growing things which depend on rain for their survival and how human beings and their cattle benefit from them. Rain makes the rivers flow, fills the lakes and keeps plants alive. It gives the purest water and there nothing wrong in drinking it. Not only human beings, but all living creatures need rain water for their growth. We must thank Allah for providing such a valuable thing.

## Lightning

The Quran says: "It is He who shows you the lightning, inspiring fear and hope" *(see Surah al-Ra'd 13:12)* On the subject of hope, scientists have discovered that when lightning slices through the atmosphere, it knocks electrons from the nitrogen atoms, which are then free to combine with oxygen and hydrogen in the atmosphere, forming nitrates. Rain carries this new compound to the earth, enriching the soil with it. These nitrates are then synthesized by plants into proteins, which can be used by animals and humans beings.

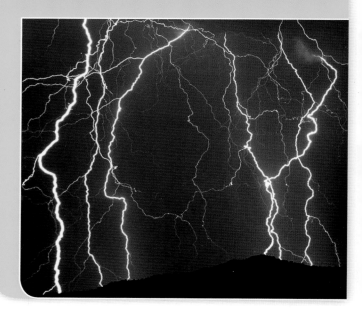

## Sun

The sun benefits the world in numerous ways. It delivers light and heat. Plants and trees get their essential nutrients from the sun. It evaporates the ground water which later comes to us as rain. Its rising and setting shows the beginning and ending of a day. The Quran says: "He causes the break of day, and has made the night for rest and He made the sun and the moon to a precise measure. That is the measure determined by the Almighty and the All Knowing." *(Surah al-An'am 6:96)*

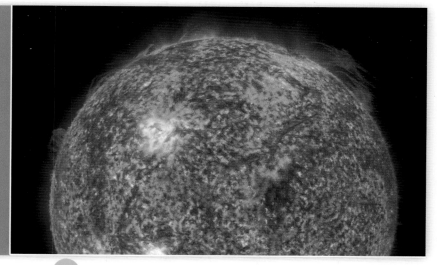

## Moon

The moon gives us cool light in the darkness of night. The moon has gravitational impact that causes tides in the ocean. Tidal waters are harnessed to produce energy. Tides also help captains to manoeuvre their ships and sail smoothly. Allah says in the Quran: "It is He who made the sun radiate a brilliant light and the moon shed its lustre, and ordained for it stages so that you may learn to count out the years and reckoning of time." *(Surah Yunus 10:5)* Muslims follow the lunar calendar which is known as the *Hijri* calendar.

## Mountains

Mountains play an important role in stabilizing the earth. They are a great source of rivers, minerals, flora and fauna. Allah says in the Quran: "We have spread out the earth, and set upon it firm mountains and caused everything to grow in due proportion. We have provided therein a means of livelihood for you and for all those creatures for whom you do not provide." *(Surah al-Nazi'at 79:30-33)*

## Stars

Like the sun and moon, the stars are part of Allah's creation. Stars were created for three prime reasons. Allah explains in the Quran: "We have adorned the lowest heaven with lamps, and We have made them for driving away devils." *(Surah al-Mulk 67:5)* Also in another verse of the Quran: "It is He who has set up for you the stars so that you might be guided by them in the midst of the darkness of land and sea. We have made the signs clear for people who want to understand." *(Surah al-An'am 6:97)*

## Oceans

Oceans are abundant sources of seafood and mineral products like, magnesium, bromine, and sodium chloride. A considerable amount of the world's petroleum production is done from the offshore oil and gas wells of the oceans. With their innumerable benefits, oceans facilitate transportation of goods and materials to support international trade and commerce between countries. Thus Allah says in the Quran: "It is He who subjected to you the sea, so that you may eat its fresh seafood and bring forth from it ornaments to wear. You see the ships cleaving through it. All this, so that you may seek His bounty and feel grateful." *(Surah al-Nahl 16:14)*

Places

# Places Mentioned in the Quran

### 1. Madinah

Madinah, known as Yathrib before the Prophet's migration there, is the second holiest city of Islam, and was only subsequently named Madinat al-Nabi (the City of the Prophet). The Prophet dearly loved Madinah and its people and it was here that he lived out his life until his death. The Prophet's Mosque (Masjid Nabawi) and his tomb lie at the city's centre. Although a visit to Madinah is not a part of Hajj, most pilgrims visit the city and offer their prayers in the Prophet's Mosque.

### 2. Madyan

The people of Madyan (between Egypt and Syria) were initially followers of the Prophet Ibrahim ﷺ, but they began over the next 500 years to adopt wrong practices in business and religion. Out of self-interest, they gave short measures and weights, thus denying others their rightful dues. The Prophet Shuayb ﷺ was sent to reform them, but they ignored him. Finally, they were all destroyed by an earthquake. When the Prophet Musa ﷺ (Moses) feared being killed by the Fir'awn (Pharaoh), he escaped from Egypt and reached Madyan, where he married a daughter of Shuayb. He lived there for some ten years.

### 3. Iram

The city of the people of 'Ad lay at the southern end of the Red Sea. The people of the city were extremely prosperous and built great palaces on the mountain tops. But because they sinned and rejected the call of the Prophet Hud ﷺ, they all were destroyed by a furious wind which Allah let loose against them for seven nights and eight days unremittingly. The Quran calls it the City of Columns. Archaeologists discovered this city in Oman and found columns to be distinctive features of this ancient city.

### 4. Jerusalem

Jerusalem, brought under Islamic rule in A.D. 638, has great sanctity in all the monotheistic religions and, in Islam, is the holiest place after Makkah and Madinah. The first *qiblah*, where the Prophet Ibrahim ﷺ (Abraham) preached, it later became the centre of activity for a succession of prophets from Ishaq (Isaac) to Isa (Jesus). For Muslims, Jerusalem derives its greatest sanctity from the Prophet Muhammad's ﷺ Night Journey (*mi'raj*), when he was brought by the Angel Jibril (Gabriel) to the Temple Mount, where he met many previous prophets and led them in prayer.

## 5. Babylon

Babil or Babylon is one of the most ancient cities, famous as the source of the science of magic. It is situated on the Euphrates River some 88 kilometers south of Baghdad. Today, the ruins of the city can be seen near the contemporary town of al-Hilla, Iraq. The Quran mentions the city with reference to the two angels, Harut and Marut, who were sent down by Allah to test and warn the people of Babil, who had begun to indulge in corrupt practices, using magic for their own benefit.

## 6. Tuwa

It was at Tuwa, at the foot of Mount Tur, that Allah spoke directly to the Prophet Musa ﷺ, bestowing upon him prophethood. While travelling from Madyan, the Prophet Musa ﷺ lost his way and asked his family to stop until he could get his bearings, or at least bring a burning brand from a fire he saw burning on the mountainside to keep them warm. But the moment he approached, Allah called out from his right side: "Musa, I am your Lord. Take off your sandals, for you are now in the sacred valley of Tuwa." *(Surah Taha 20:9:14)*

## 8. The Thaqif

The Thaqif is one of the major tribes which are mentioned in the Quran. In 628 A.D., the Prophet Muhammad left Makkah for Taif with his family. He went there to give the message of Islam and to look for the support of the townspeople. The people of Taif belonged to the Thaqif tribe. They not only refused to support him but insulted him. They threw stones at him and badly injured him.

## 7. Makkah

Makkah, called the Mother of Cities in the Quran, is Islam's holiest city, towards which prayers are said five times every day by over a quarter of the world's population. Located in a valley in the Sirat Mountains 70 miles from the Red Sea coast of Saudi Arabia, Makkah derives its importance from the Kabah, which Allah ordered the Prophet Ibrahim ﷺ to build, and also from the birth there of the Prophet Muhammad ﷺ, who brought the message of Islam. Millions of Muslims from different parts of the world travel each year to this holy city to perform their Hajj and *Umrah*.

## 9. Tubba

The Quran mentions the people of Tubba twice. Tubba is understood to be a title or family name of the Himyar kings in Yemen of the Hamdan tribe. The Himyar were ancient race. The individual Tubba spoken in the Quran was a believer, but his people were wrongdoers and hence were destroyed. Their earliest religion was Sabianism or the worship of the heavenly bodies.

## 10. Hudaybiyyah

Hudaybiyyah, is a place which lies some nine miles away from Makkah. Here, in the sixth year of Hijrah, the Prophet Muhammad ﷺ was stopped by the Quraysh while on his way from Madinah along with 1400 of his Companions to perform *Umrah* at Makkah. The Prophet camped here and waited for about two weeks, during which time he began having talks with the Quraysh leaders to avoid a fight. Ultimately, the famous peace treaty was signed here, which is referred to in the Quran as an 'obvious victory'.

# Landscapes

## 1 Mount Uhud

Mount Uhud is a volcanic hill on the western outskirts of Madinah. This mountain is of a great historical importance. The famous historic battle of Uhud was fought near this mountain in the third year of Hijrah, in which a number of the Companions were martyred, including the Prophet's uncle Hamzah. The Prophet himself was wounded on his head and face, and one of his front teeth was broken. The graves of the martyrs are still shown here.

## 2 Mount Sinai

Located in the Central Sinai Peninsula in Egypt, Mount Sinai is also known as Jabal Musa, or the Mountain of Moses. While travelling with his family, the Prophet Musa ﷺ saw a burning bush on the mountainside and asked his family to wait while he brought a burning brand from it. But when he reached it, a voice called out: "O Musa! I am Allah, the Lord of the World." Here Musa was shown great miracles and he was given the Tawrat (the Ten Commandments and the Law).

## 3 The Nile

The Nile River is believed to be the longest river in the world. Emerging from East Africa, it flows through Kenya, Eritrea, Congo, Burundi, Uganda, Tanzania, Rwanda, Egypt, Sudan and Ethiopia to the Mediterranean. The Nile River has great significance in regard to ancient Egypt. According to a hadith recorded in Sahih al-Bukhari, it is one of the two worldly rivers found in *jannah* (paradise), the other being the Euphrates. This river is referred to in many verses in the Quran.

## 4 Arafat Mountain

Arafat Mountain, situated within the holy precincts of Makkah, is a major meeting point for the Hajj. On the 9th Dhu'l Hijjah, more than two million pilgrims go there from Makkah and Mina for the *wuquf*—the standing of 'Arafat' — the most essential part of the Hajj. As the Prophet Muhammad ﷺ said, "The (day of) 'Arafat is the Hajj'. The focal point is the 200 feet high Mount of Mercy (Jabal al-Rahmah), from which in A.D. 632 the Prophet preached his last sermon — the Khutbah of the Hajjat al-Wida" (Sermon of the Farewell Hajj).

## 6 Mount Judi

For decades archeological teams have tried to unearth the Ark of the Prophet Nuh عليه السلام from beneath the snowy snow and ice of Mount Judi, a 7,700 foot high mountain in present-day Kurdistan. Finally, in early 1994, a team of scientists and archaeologists found what they firmly believed could be the remains of the Prophet Nuh's Ark. The most striking fact is that as early as 1400 years ago, the Quran mentioned this very spot as the Ark's final resting place.

## 7 The River of the Paradise

In *Surah al-Kawthar* in the Quran, God announces to the Prophet: "We have given you the Kawthar." (A heavenly river). Of this river, the Prophet once observed: "Its breadth and width is the distance of one month's journey; on its two banks are tents made of hollow pearls, its smell is better than musk, its water is whiter than milk and its taste is sweeter than honey; its drinking vessels are as numerous as the stars in the sky. Whoever drinks from it, will never be thirsty again."

## 8 The Cave of Thawr

The Cave of Thawr is where the Prophet Muhammad ﷺ and his closest Companion, Abu Bakr, hid for three nights on their migration from Makkah to Madinah. It is located on the Jabal (Mount) Thawr on the southern outskirts of Makkah, some 14 km away from the city of Makkah. When the search party of pagan Makkan came near the cave, Abu Bakr became frightened. But, according to the Quran, the Prophet said calmly: "Do not despair, Allah is with us." *(Surah al-Tawbah 9:40)*

## 9 The Cave of Hira

The Cave of Hira is the place where the first revelation of the Quran was made to the Prophet Muhammad ﷺ. This cave is situated on the summit of Jabal al-Nur (the Mountain of Light) to the north east of Makkah, a few miles away from the city on the road to Mina. There the Prophet would retreat to think about the creation of Allah. Khadija, his wife, would send him food, so that he could remain in the cave for several days at a stretch.

## 10 Safa and Marwah

Safa and Marwah are two hillocks situated near the Kabah. According to the Quran, they are signs of Allah. Those performing Hajj or *umrah*, walk seven times between these two hillocks, starting from Safa and ending at Marwah. This walking is called *sa'i*. *Sa'i* is performed in remembrance of Hajar's running back and forth between these two hillocks in search of water to quench the thirst of her son Ismail.

# Makkah

### 1. Maqam Ibrahim

Maqam Ibrahim means the Station of Ibrahim or the Standing Place of the Prophet Ibrahim علیہ السلام. A small kiosk in the immediate vicinity of Kabah contains a stone which is traditionally believed to be the stone on which the Prophet Ibrahim علیہ السلام and his son Ismail stood while building the Kabah. The Quran urges believers to take Maqam Ibrahim as a place of prayer. A two *rakah* prayer is offered here during Hajj and *Umrah*.

### 2. Allah Saved the Kabah

During the time of the grandfather of the Prophet, Abdul Muttalib, a Yemeni King known as Abraha, had built a grand temple at Sana and wanted this to be the pilgrimage centre. He was envious of the status of the Kabah among the people. So he decided to destroy the Kabah and led an army of elephants to Makkah. However, his army was destroyed by flock of birds who pelted them with *sijjin* (baked clay) before he could reach the Kabah. In this way, Allah saved the Kabah. It is mentioned in the Quran in *Surah al-Fil,* as the story of the People of the Elephant (Ashab-e-fil).

### 3. The City of Blessings

Makkah is the holiest place in Islam because the Kabah, the first House of Worship appointed for mankind by Allah, is situated here. According to the Quran, the city is full of blessings and whosoever enters Makkah attains security. Makkah is surrounded by mountains and is 70 km inland from the Red Sea coast of Saudi Arabia. Millions of Muslims from different parts of the world travel each year to this holy city to perform Hajj and *Umrah*.

### 4. Blessed Land

Makkah is a blessed place. The superiority of Makkah has been explicitly mentioned in many places in the Quran. And according to a *hadith*, the Prophet said: "By Allah, you are the best land of Allah, the most beloved land of Allah. Had I not been driven out of you, I would not have left you." The reward for praying in Makkah is multiplied many times over. According to a *hadith*, a single prayer in Makkah is better than one hundred thousand prayers elsewhere.

## 5. The Mountains of Makkah

Makkah is situated in a rugged, rocky, predominantly granite terrain, with mountain ranges on three sides, to the west, south and east. Jabal al Nur and Jabal al Thawr are located in these mountain ranges. Both places are very important from historical point of view.

## 6. Makkah in the Quran

Makkah is mentioned in the Quran by different names. The Quran calls it Makkah in *Surah al- Fath* (48:24), *Al-Qaryah* in *Surah an- Nahl* (16:112) and in Surah 90, Allah swears by this city and calls it *al-Balad*. It is also mentioned as *Ummul Qura* and Bakkah.

## 7. The Black Stone

The black stone in the Kabah is said to be the stone which was fixed by the Prophet Ibrahim ﷵ when he was building the Kabah. When the Quraysh were rebuilding the Kabah at the time of the Prophet Muhammad ﷺ, they chose the Prophet to put the black stone in its place.

## 8. The First House of Worship

The Kabah is the first house of worship. Allah says in the Quran: "Verily , the first House (of Worship) appointed for mankind was that at Bakkah (Makkah), full of blessing, and a guidance for all people". It was first built by the Prophet Ismail ﷵ and the Prophet Ibrahim ﷵ.

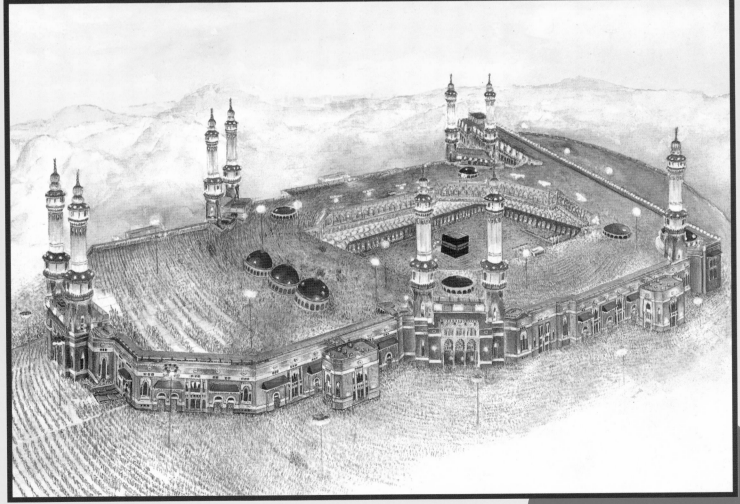

# Madinah

## 1 The City of Madinah

The city of Madinah is a blessed place to which the Prophet Muhammad ﷺ migrated from Makkah. Allah commanded the Prophet to migrate to the city of Madinah: The Quran says: "And say (O Muhammad): My Lord ! Let my entry (into the city of Madinah) be good and (likewise) my exit (from the city of Makkah) be good."

## 2 An Important Pledge

The Prophet Muhammad ﷺ used to preach Islam to those who would come to Makkah on Hajj. So, some tribes of Madinah converted to Islam when the Prophet introduced Islam to them while they were on Hajj. Subsequently, these tribes also pledged to support Islam and the Prophet. This pledge is famously known as the Pledge of Aqabah.

## 3 Al-Muallim

When a large number of people from Madinah came into the fold of Islam, the Prophet thought of sending somebody from Makkah to teach Islam to them. The Prophet Muhammad ﷺ sent Mus'ab Bin Umayr, one of the Companions, there to teach Islam before his migration.

## 4 The Migration to Madinah

The Makkans were conspiring to kill the Prophet. So, he was commanded by Allah to migrate to Madinah. The angel Jibril came to the Prophet and told him to leave Makkah and migrate to Madinah. The Prophet Muhammad ﷺ left Makkah with Abu Bakr in the dead of night. And that night, Ali Ibn Abu Talib, his cousin, slept at his place, when some of the Quraysh attacked the Prophet's house.

## 5 Jannat al-Baqi

In Madinah, there is an important graveyard situated to the east of the Prophet's mosque. It is known as Jannat al-Baqi. Based on the sayings of the Prophet, this graveyard has many virtues. The Prophet's wife A'isha said that whenever the Prophet would stay in her house, he would go in the last part of the night to this graveyard. The Prophet's wife, A'isha too is buried here.

## 6 The First Friday Prayer

The Prophet prayed his first Friday prayer before entering Madinah in the middle of a valley known as Ranuqna. This place belonged to the tribe of the Banu Salim bin Awf. This mosque is known as Masjid-e-Juma.

## 7 The First Mosque

Before entering the city of Madinah, the Prophet Muhammad ﷺ stayed at a place called Quba where a mosque was later built. It was inhabited by the tribe of Banu Amr bin Awf. This mosque is known as Masjid-e-Quba.

## 8 Virtues of Madinah

The city of Madinah has special distinction. It is the city where the Prophet Muhammad migrated to from Makkah. Allah made this place special because the Prophet supplicated for the well being of its inhabitants. According to a hadith, the Prophet encouraged people to live in Madinah. The Prophet prayed to Allah: "O Allah make Madinah beloved to us, as we love Makkah -- or more..." The Prophet also said that none would go out of the city with a dislike of it.

## 9 Al-Qiblatayn Mosque

A revelation from Allah came to the Prophet to change the Qibla while he was praying in a mosque in Madinah at the Banu Salamah village. Later this mosque was named al-Qiblatayn Mosque.

## 10 Al-Fath Mosque

During the Battle of the Trench the Prophet prayed on a mountainside for three days. Allah finally heard his prayer and the glad tidings of victory were revealed to him. This mosque is today known as Al Fath mosque. It is located on Mount Sala.

Jerusalem ⟫

# Jerusalem

## 1 The City of Jerusalem

Jerusalem is a holy city blessed by Allah. The city of Jerusalem is known in Arabic as Al-Quds or Baitul-Maqdis (the noble, sacred place). Many Prophets lived in this blessed land. The Prophet Sulayman ﷺ, who had power over the Jinn, the birds, the wind and the animals, ruled from here. It is situated in the Middle East near Jordan and Syria. Jerusalem has many sites of Islamic significance such as Masjid al-Aqsa, the Dome of the Rock, Masjid Umar, etc. It is reported that the Prophet Muhammad ﷺ said, "There are only three mosques to which you should embark on a journey: the sacred mosque, this mosque of mine, and the mosque of Al-Aqsa (Jerusalem)."

## 3 The Prophet's Night Journey

In the tenth year of prophethood the angel Jibril came to take the Prophet Muhammad ﷺ on the miraculous journey from Makkah to Jerusalem and then to the heavens. At Jerusalem, the Prophet Muhammad ﷺ said his prayers at the Farthest Mosque (al-Masjid al-Aqsa), where all other prophet joined him in prayer. It happened in 621 A.D. That night the Prophet was staying in the house of Umm Hani, the daughter of Abi Talib at Makkah.

## 2 The Farthest Mosque

The Quran mentions the Farthest Mosque to which the Prophet Muhammad ﷺ was taken and where he led a *salah* of the prophets. A mosque was later built on this site. Today, it is known as Al-Aqsa Mosque. Its construction was started by Abd al-Malik and it was completed by his predecessor, Al-Walid.

### 4  The Ascension

Al-Mir'aj means the ascension. From Jerusalem the Prophet Muhammad ﷺ ascended to the heavens accompanied by the angel Jibril. The Prophet ascended up the seven heavens, one by one. He met prophets in each heaven. He met the Prophet Adam عليه السلام, the forefather of man, in the first heaven. The Prophet Yahya عليه السلام and Isa عليه السلام in the second heaven, the Prophet Yusuf عليه السلام in the third, the Prophet Idris عليه السلام in the fourth, the Prophet Harun عليه السلام in the fifth and the Prophet Musa عليه السلام in the sixth. When the Prophet Muhammad ﷺ came back home, he was amazed to find the spot where he had lain was still warm, and the cup he had tipped over was still emptying. This incredible experience had taken place in less than a moment.

### 6  The Dome of the Rock

The Prophet had climbed upon a rock at Bayt al Maqdis from where he was taken to the heavens. A special structure was later built at this place. It is called the Dome of the Rock and it is sacred to Jews, Christian and Muslims alike. It was, in fact, the original prayers direction (qiblah) of the early Muslims before the direction of Makkah replaced it in the second year of the Hijrah. The Dome of the Rock was built by Abd al-Malik. The rock itself is oblong and measures 56 feet by 42 feet. Below it is a chamber accessible by a stairway where one can pray in a small area set aside for the purpose.

### 5  Hebron

As commanded by Allah the Prophet Ibrahim عليه السلام traveled to different places. Before moving to Egypt, he settled in Jerusalem with his family. He is buried in Hebron, a small place near Jerusalem.

### 7  A Gift for the Ummah

The Prophet Muhammad ﷺ was given a beautiful gift for his Ummah when he went on al-Mir'aj. This gift is called Miftahul Jannah. Allah gave him the gift of Salah or daily prayer. Originally, fifty daily prayers had been ordained, but the prophet Musa عليه السلام asked him to return and ask for a reduction. First the prayers were reduced to 10 and then finally to five.

Index ▶▶▶

# Index

Picture Credits: tc03; tl, br45; tl, bl, cr61; cr07; tr62, tr63; [S.M. Amin; Abdullah Y. Al-Dobais; Thomas Sennett; Tom McNeff & Jerry Herring; David H. Wells respectively for *Saudi Aramco World/SAWDIA*]
Others: tr03, cr06, bl6, cl44, tr45, cl54, tr55, bl55, br56, cr57, cl60.
The rest of the images are used under license from *123rf.com*.

"Your Lord inspired the bee, saying, 'Make your homes in the mountains, in the trees, and also in the structures which men erect. Then feed on every kind of fruit, and follow the trodden paths of your Lord.' From its belly comes a drink with different colours which provides healing for mankind. Indeed, in this there is a sign for people who give thought."

*Surah Al-Nahl, 16:68*